UNCOMMON
Grace

UNCOMMON
Grace

Jasmine Strange

UNCOMMON GRACE
ISBN-13: 978-0692872925

For speaking engagements, book the author at:
strangefundamentals@yahoo.com

Published by: Jasmine Strange

Printed in the United States of America
Charleston, SC

Cover Photo: Jim Payton
Through God's Eye Photography

Inspiration

Nikki Giovanni, Iyanla Vanzant and Maya Angelou

Thank you for instilling the power of writing, expression and the gift of a story unfolded to the world to me.

Devon Franklin and John Singleton

Devon Franklin, author of *Produced by Faith, The Wait,* producer of the movie *Woodlawn* and *Miracles from Heaven.* He has also worked on movies such as *Karate Kid* and *The Pursuit of Happiness* John Singleton, film director of movies such as *Boyz in the Hood, Baby Boy, Poetic Justice, Four Brothers, Higher Learning* and more, would be the other in a matter of years that I would come into contact with, long enough to hear *his story.*

These two men showed me the power of standing in what you believe to be true as God has called and pre-destined for my life. They showed me in real time, that destiny is written by our creative ability and is walked out by faith. *Eye opening* to say the least! Their lives have paved the way and given hope, encouragement and motivation to so many of us that follow.

These are men that are living and currently working in their perspective fields, not passed on and in a history book for us to research their lives, leaving us to guess the if's, who's, where's, when's, how's and why's. No. They stood in my face as an open book and allowed me in. They allowed the world to see, feel, hope, dream, be and do! My God!

I thank them, for they have released into the world, a power that they may and may never know. Nevertheless, their selflessness has freed many and birthed much!

As a seed is planted, its roots grow long…Words from an upcoming single of mine, "Live Again". These two men have roots that extend far past even generations to come. My children have watched the product of their once visions. I have lived them. Seeds not yet here, will carry them out. How much deeper rooted can you get? Devon left me with the strength and courage, as he says, "It's best to be successful without losing yourself; that your belief system follows you. Sit down and have a business meeting with yourself," he said. "Plan out a guide for your life and begin by taking your first step."

John left me with much more than I can write on today, but that the creative mind was never meant to fit in. It is not supposed to. A creative mind creates something from nothing. It is ok to be different. Different is what makes you, *You!*

I left both encounters with my chest stuck out far, head held high and swag in my step. Lol...These men are the visionaries you can only pray to cross paths within this world.

Pastor John Gregg of Calvary Temple in Pittsburg, California, once said, "If you desire to be successful, you must align yourself with positive visionaries." God aligned me with these two men and so many more. There is no other way I could fathom such favor happening in a lifetime. To this day, I know that I am walking in *Uncommon Grace*!

Table of Contents

"Your gift to you, is to love you with the love of God. (John 13:34) Loving self is not an arrogant or prideful position. It is a position that simply says, "I'm too good for that." If we aren't basing our thoughts and emotions on what represents our worth, our wisdom and our potential, we have to stop and realize that something is wrong beloved. When thoughts and decisions habitually disagree with self-love, something is wrong beloved. Growth means that there are some things, behaviors and even some people that should no longer be tolerable or acceptable. If we're still tolerating the intolerable, growth is necessary." – Dr. Patrick Weaver, Abundant Life Christian Ministries.

Funny how our lives represented on paper tells such a different story from that of a fly on the wall...

We share what we want to share, say what we want to say, show what we want to show,

And only what we want, do we actually reveal

To feel what we want to feel

In this way we are able to hide behind a painted mask

Giving off the heir of..." I DARE YOU TO ASK!"

Living in bondage, like a slave

Taking our stories straight to the grave

So yeah we may shine for but a moment

Selling our souls to the side of the opponent

Sound crazy to you????

But that's what we do!

We walk past the young girl who's looking at you

Afraid she might find out ALL you've been through

BUT...ISN'T THAT THE POINT???

WE ARE LIVING TESTIMONIES!

Our lives we lay down

Shedding our old man ... to wear a crown

He died for us, don't let him down

That young girl needs you, to see her way through

So guide her and love her and tell her your truth

My name is Jasmine a sinner by race

What you see now is His Uncommon Grace

Introduction

I've always believed as a woman, I'd have a pretty good package to present one day to the man of my dreams. I was pretty, clean, had a good heart, smart, friendly, loyal; Beginning to sound like an ad for a free puppy?

I could cook a little and although great with children, I had none. I had proven to be a great team player and as trusting as they came…naive would be the better word, but that was ok because I would be protected by the man that was going to love me for life right? I was confident this was not something I needed to be worried about. The only thing I foresaw having to do would be the hiring of a maid; an ugly one that is (kidding). Truthfully, however, cleanliness as some say though next to Godliness, has never been my forte'. I'm working on it.

Somewhere along my journey, through all of my experiences, I took a left turn and had a shift in my belief of who I was and what exactly I really did have to offer a man or anybody for that matter. I don't know where it started or where I got it from, but I began to feel as though the greatest thing I had to offer a man now was my body. I knew how much a woman's body was desired. Our temples are sacred. We belong to God and are not to be touched until marriage.. So I believed

i

if I gave my body to them, seeing as though it belonged to God, I was giving them the ultimate gift; myself! They'd come to see how much I really loved them, giving them something that belonged to God, that is. Absolute *foolishness*, I know. It is my desire in this book to be as truthful as I can that you, along with myself, may learn from my ill-minded, idiocrasies up until this point. The point in which I found God for myself....

"The point that Jesus steps in, you will have life, obtain favor and prosper!", this is what my Bishop, Christopher C. Smith would always remind me during sermons at church..

What I came to find is that this ludicrous mindset that I had been operating in did not show men how much I loved them. Instead, it showed them how little I loved myself and that I had placed them above God. Even the devil knew this was silly. Can you say field day? "I don't hear nobody! Pastor Wiley would say. Yes, a *Field Day*! This is what the enemy would have with my life for the next some ought years. I had given so much of myself, that it had very little value to me or the next man. You see, the jacked up value system and mindset that I had acquired made it easy for a man to get what he desired of me without accounting for moral or biblical principles. However, being an easy catch was not what was most attractive to men. It was simply what was easiest.

I would later come to find out just what would attract a man to a woman he could, one day, claim as his own. A God-fearing man wants a woman that he can bring into his life to walk by his side, bring home to momma and cherish and value forever. A woman with the moral values strong enough to hold back and say *no*! A woman that would wait until God revealed her "Boaz" to her; she to her "Boaz" to love by way of His Word. Love, marriage, then sex. Love meaning, God and all that His Word stands for. If they can follow the direction and guidance of the Master, he can wait for you. In loving God, he will also have that much more respect for you because he will see you as God's daughter and not the devil's slaughter. In loving God, you will be able to truly begin to love you too.

Embarrassed and hurt; two of the many words I have been feeling since this revelation took place. Several of the men I have been with, I now see on Facebook, or even at times in public happily engaged with that specially chosen woman in their life. Sometimes holding hands, laughing and smiling, swapping stares of endearment, some even married. Never the less, they are publicly showing, giving and displaying, affection, respect and love for these women. Get this, even shown enjoying time with one another before 11pm at night! I thought that was only in the movies, but it's not. It actually happens in real life and not because they need a meal or a place to stay. It is possible to love and be loved. These same men wouldn't know me from "Eve" in the daytime; at least that's what they'd have the public to believe. But there is hope!

With all just stated, I failed to realize that there are principals to be mindful of packaged or coupled with living right. Tithing is but one principal we learn of in the Bible, however, you can pay your tithes and offering, give of your time, and even your talents, but if you are not following the Word of the God, the light will eventually dim as hope turns into despair. Upon a change in mind and heart, it is possible to be victorious in God. What does victory look like?

➤ Giving your life over to Jesus

➤ Knowing you serve a God who can do all things

➤ Confidence that you have victory in Him no matter what it looks like

➤ Serving a God Who says you can when you've doubted your entire life the possibility that you could

➤ Knowing where your strength comes from

➤ The confirmation that God lives inside of you

➤ Seeing how far you've come by way of the mighty works He has done through you

➤ Never competing for love. God is love. It is His free gift to you, one in which He has paid His life for.

Because He died and rose again, *we win*!

Even if you aren't chosen by a man or a woman, there is always a spot for you Queen or King, in God's court and on His team in the Kingdom. I know if there's a place for me, surely there's a place for you! This is one of the lines in my first released single, *Praisn' All by Myself.*

This book is written as a healing tool for myself in which prayerfully you will gain as well. It is my desire that in being honest with myself and you with my tarnished past, I will begin to find freedom by way of taking hold to the Word of God as I journey to a place called now. In knowing Him, I begin to learn myself and the authentic call He has placed on my life. In other words, I will awaken to myself as I awaken to His desired purpose for my life.

I've come to understand that it is selfish of me not to share that which ultimately almost consumed my soul. I pray all, especially young women, will not judge what I have to say but rather receive that which has saved my soul. I wish to be consumed by nothing but the Word of God that has given me life! It is said that the healing power of God is to be shared. Since He healed me, Surely He can heal *you* too! (Psalm 32:1-8)

CHAPTER ONE

The Dirty Dirt

To know where you come from helps in knowing why you are the way you are. It is the sum of our total experiences that make up who we are but in no way is the final determinate of who we will become. To begin to unlock the door to our future, we must first give light to the past that it may not be repeated. I was raised an only child by a single African-American mother, who was a tenacious mix of, Swedish, Choctaw and Blackfoot Indian.

I watched her daily struggle to maintain a life for me that was conducive to a hopeful productive outcome. I thought to myself many times what a highly intellectual, educated, skilled and courageous woman of God she was. She was both a walking encyclopedia and Bible. An English Professor to heart, a writer for the Oakland Tribune, college professor and circuit speaker oftentimes called to travel the states to speak, teach and train leaders in various fields. You can only imagine what some of our daily conversations consisted of. I remember the conversations that took place in our humble abode.

Jasmine ... you never place a preposition at the end of a sentence! Now what were you saying? Many times I fumbled and bumbled over her grand expectations of what now I'm ever so grateful for. I was unable to get across my true thoughts, my feelings, my inner lady, at the time little girl. My self-expression muted because of my elementary communication skills. I felt as though I would never compare, add up or even make it to her level of achievement, let alone surpass it as I've heard so many say that children are supposed to do from one generation to the next.

Between the ages of eleven and twelve, my eyes began to open to the world. I had begun to walk to school with my cousins; an independence we greatly appreciated! We briefly explored the world together. This was a time in my life I will cherish forever. Along with our special moments in time, came an abundance of fun coupled with many days of shared discipline. As much as I enjoyed my time hanging with them seeing as though I was an only child. It posed quite a different challenge than the one found in my household. You see, there were five of them! Back in the 80's, we were the first 6 of what today has now grown to 14 not including our own children which brings the grandchildren and great grandchildren count to a total of 30 and counting. Though today we are spread all over the states and even country at times, we were for a brief moment in time inseparable. I remember situations where spankings were necessary for events that occurred in the innocence of our childhood. However, due to the number of us, it was always difficult to tell just who the recipient of punishment should truly be. None of us dare tell on one another or was it that we all told on each other? Well, not sure how your households' ran, but in theirs, we all had to line up and face the music! This would be to the tune and rhythm played out on our behinds! I love them all so dearly. We all turned out ok. Lol...the most amazing people you will ever meet and I don't say that because they are my cousins.

Shortly thereafter, I would begin my first job! Babysitting! My mother connected me with a woman in the building in which we lived who later became my modeling coach. She had a young son of whom they entrusted me to take care of. This would include escorting him to and from school on the public transportation system; the city bus! This venture would last until... the day I got off of the bus as we were in route home from school, only to turn around and find that my little counterpart was no longer with me! I panicked! I called my mother and told her he was missing. My mother jumped into action as we moms' do and calmly took hold of the reins. She called the bus company who initially reported that they had not seen him. The sickest feeling came over me. That was a lot of weight and responsibility for me to carry. I did not look forward to being an adult. Come to find out, the little boy had fallen asleep at the back of the bus. No one knew he was even there until the bus driver did a walk through after receiving a call from the bus dispatcher that my mom had contacted. He was curled up in a fetal position laid over on the seat exhausted from a long day at school. If you hadn't guessed, this would be my first and last job for a while!

I was being exposed daily to all sorts of new things; feelings I didn't quite understand. It was in that year I'd begin my period. I remember a meeting being held in my living room between my grandmother, my mother and a couple of aunts all talking about the news of my cycle having started as I lay in bed aching. I was miserable at best. I couldn't understand the joy they were experiencing in the other room of my crossing over into womanhood. I'd just assume stay the way I was, but not so. Nothing in life remains the same; Everything in life changes. I can remember going to parties with my mom having no babysitter and all, she would have me with her as I wondered through the crowd and eventually outdoors and onto the street where I had no business. Down the street I'd go exploring life even if only a block or two away. I'd get whistled at, mind you I was only 11 or 12 years old. I can recall grown men passing by on the street saying . . . mmm, mmm, I'll be back for you when you grow up. Not knowing quite how to process comments like these at the time, I held them in my head knowing they had some sort of relevance to the drawing power a girl could have over a man. I looked forward to one day finding out its full pulling power.

I had not the slightest idea I'd be the one getting pulled, right into a whirlwind of depression, confusion, embarrassment, despair, and so many other detrimental emotions. I wasn't equipped to properly deal with what would come next. I was blossoming quite rapidly and the growing pains ailing me. Boys became my *focal* point. I had somehow connected with one I'd eventually write letters to in jail. This didn't help in the rearing process my Mom was now facing.

It wasn't long that the apparent hardship of becoming a single mommy, after the dream of marriage and the responsibility of having done it all right, only to fall short (what was falling short anyhow?) . . . kicked in. There was heaviness in spirit that I soon felt surrounded by. What did I know? I was only a child. However, as a young single mother now myself, this is how I've come to see it in relation to what it was back then. I still hear my mom speak endearingly of my father even after some ought 40 years. I pray to meet a man that will touch my heart in that way as well.

Today, I can feel a space in her heart. I ponder over what exactly makes for a successful union. There is no picture book blueprint of an example. She, unlike me, at least tried to do it the right way, the way of the Good Book.

Still, I imagine this was not the life a college graduate, Masters educated and soon to be doctorate recipient, would even conceive of living. However, this had become her reality. The strain eventually pushed us into a period of separation. Everything I did, from that point forward, I felt had to be even more on point, above board, as they say. I believe the intent was no different from many single moms or parents desiring to raise their children to thrive in the best capacity possible. The strain was tough, almost unbearable. A period of separation; inevitable. Everything I did or said, I felt was on spotlight. Daily I must have reminded her of my father or at least what she thought his role was to be in our lives but was no longer. Of course, this was not his plan to be separated from us, but this too would be his reality as well. Subsequently, the school district in Oakland went on strike. As the educator she was, my mother was not having the sit at home watching cartoons and eating bowls of cereal as I had intended my days would encompass for the next couple of weeks, even possibly months. So I was sent to Pittsburg, California, to live with my grandparents and finish out my seventh grade year. It was this year that I would be introduced to sex! This would be when my life would forever change.

As if the strain was not on thick enough, the dimension this threw me in would be one in which has taken a lifetime to recover from. This book is a product of a recovering soul.. The fight of my life. The desire to save a soul; my soul, your soul, any soul, that it may not be totally consumed, unless by God. I, like most, had begun to live out my life's purpose without even realizing it. We live and continue to live until our purpose is made manifest. We either accept it or reject it. Fight up stream or flow with it.

Living with grandma, I had freedoms I didn't otherwise have at home. I was able to walk home with my best friend Sheen and her twin brother Eric, who I always had a crush on. We were inseparable; Sheen and I. I have far too many stories to share between hiding my report cards in the bushes on the way home from school to forming our own rap and dance group. If this weren't a book, I'd give you a sample! Oh yes! I still remember my part! We'd even sneak away to the opposing junior high school in town to attend their dances because they were much cooler than ours, so we thought. Well, I snuck. They probably had permission. At one particular dance, I was close to being jumped for kissing an ex-boyfriend of a girl who had one of the biggest families in town! I think they must have all been there that night too! Lol ...Whew! Thank God I got out of there alive! "Computer Love" would be the last song I heard before my friends rushed me out of there! I will never forget those days and I will never forget my friends. We remain in contact to this very day, children grown and our hearts turned to the Lord. We shared some of the best, and what felt to be worst, times of our lives. In fact, it would be my best friend Sheen that I frantically called just before my first sexual experience occurred that following summer. I don't know if I was more afraid or nervous, but I knew something was about to take place and I didn't know what to do.

The attempt to find myself due to my inconsistent and unstable living conditions in my life didn't help, although it was not all to blame. When the year was over, I returned to stay with my aunt for the summer and help to take care of her children, gain a little freedom from the stresses at home and make a little money. This, too, would be a turning point in the relationship with one of seven of my mother's siblings, my aunt, as the introduction of the sexual encounter would, unbeknownst to her, take place on her watch and under her care. From the get go, my relationships with boys and men have been dysfunctional and all of the introductions since then, improper. I was 13, he 17. To make matters worse, he was my aunt's new husband's little half-brother. As the child that I was, having just turned 13 that month, I had not taken into consideration any of the lasting affects this would have on me. This would affect my immediate family, him, his family, my future and my children that would eventually come. Unfortunately, my children are still suffering from mistakes I made almost 28 years ago. Many family relationships have never been the same. I can't help but to feel this played a large role, let alone the impact this may have had on my aunt and her new and now estranged husband and his family.

The list of infected and affected people and situations goes on. The boy, being that he was almost 18, was close to statutory rape charges, had my family had it their way and had I complied. However, I wouldn't because, of course, this was now the love of my life, right?

Nothing was ever the same. I moved back to Oakland feeling exiled and tried to continue a normal 8th grade year. It was everything but normal! It didn't matter that I was class President, Citywide counsel representative for the junior high school bracket, had received the principal's award, captain of my cheerleading squad, most popular girl, selected to represent the school, and singing at an engagement Jesse Jackson would attend. I even gave the class speech for the graduating class of 1989. I lived in pain, shame, guilt, hurt, and inadequacy. I was good at this; wearing the mask, that is. You would have never known I had any issues whatsoever. But I did, lots of them.

Regardless of my issues and shortcomings, I always had a love for God, and desired to know more of Him. That's why I began attending church on my own, even when my exhausted mother could not.

I began to pull out my eyelashes and later my eyebrows. As an early adolescent school-aged female, you can imagine this affected my morale greatly. I covered it by the use and application of heavy black make-up on my eyes. This would be applied on the way to school, as I would get off of the elevator on the 4th floor and use the community restroom. This, too, would serve as my superman or woman, for that matter, phone booth. Here, I would also change into my second set of clothes; clothing that was not seen and/or approved by my mother prior to my leaving home in the morning.

Reversing this situation to return home in the same manner in which I left came with great challenge and one day failed. My mother's car would break down on this specific day and she would then climb aboard a bus in which I was riding home from school. My heart? In my shoes! My hands? Frantically trying to scrape whatever make up I had left on my face, off! My mind? Wishing like all get out that these clothes could and would magically change back to what they were when I left the house; especially *her* shoes that were on *my* feet! Challenging years I tell you. Regardless to what I felt was unfair treatment toward me as a teenager, I didn't make the situation much easier by my adolescent style in behavior.

I would go into my moms' purse, get some money and catch the A.C. Transit bus from 1st Street all the way down E. 14th Street until I reached 84th Street in Oakland, California. I would get off at Allen Temple Baptist Church where Pastor J. Alfred Smith was my Pastor. Unfortunately, I did not always make it in the doors. Well, I take that back. I was a smart enough kid to go and check in so that people would see me and say yes, Jasmine was here. After I made my appearance, I'd end up down the street and around the corner where, once again, I had no business. Dibbling and dabbling in new found experiences similar to those I had recently encountered in that summer prior. This led to even more of a strain on the relationship with my mom and I. Later that year I'd run away.

Things had hit the fan! The unimaginable thought of my mom's young daughter having crossed into adulthood in the most inappropriate and untimely way was more than she could bare or should have to. We went head to head. I thought that night I just may lose my life. She was just that mad. We lived in a high rise off of Lake Merritt on the 24th floor. All I could think of was flying over that balcony and down 24 flights of stairs. So, I ran to Lake Merritt Bakery, which was all of a block away. Of course that would never happen, a teens mind...I tell you! Thank God for years of maturation to come., Heart pounding and body shaking after the heated altercation we had . . . one of the many, and the last if I could help it. We were, at that time, always in some sort of altercation as many teen/parent relationships can attest to. I even remember a school picture I have in which I am smiling but my sweater is ripped from a fight early that morning between my mom and I. She swung and I swung back. It was ugly! I was so ashamed for even raising my hand. I wanted to talk, not fight. I needed a hug, not a hit. I lived in false happiness and constant pain, but that was still no excuse for me to return the swing.

I called my Dad, who lived in Chicago at the time, and he connected with relatives out here on his side who would come to rescue me as I saw it. Daddy to the rescue was my mindset.

Therapy was inevitable, which my mom requested. I refused seeing as though I had not yet finished 8th grade, I had to go somewhere to see that it be accomplished before the decision to move full time to Illinois with my father. During the in between time, I stayed with yet another aunt who was in college herself raising her little boy as a single mom. Whew! Looking back, I didn't realize what a challenge that must have been for her. We made the best of it! Cheese enchilada nights and Michael Jackson Marathon weekends. Graduation Day came and went with a long graduate robe, cake, party and fake smiles. I was still living in pain, now uncertainty, guilt, and defeat. Emotions were adding up and weighing me down like a thousand-pound rock. However, I was becoming a professional at tucking away my experiences up until this age. But now a new phase of my life would begin after graduation, as I boarded the aircraft, never to look back again, or at least that was my thought.

CHAPTER TWO

I Almost Lost a Leg!

By the time I arrived in Illinois, I had the weight of the world, as it felt, on my shoulders. It was beginning to show but not fully. Though I had a head of beautiful hair and a set of full eyebrows, I had no eyelashes left. A constant reminder of what I'd gone through. My coping mechanism apparently was to pick my eyelashes out one by one. I've done it so long to this day, they are non-existent along with my eyebrows. With no make-up on, I looked as if I had undergone chemotherapy. This is a side of me that I've never really publicly availed. My father, an army vet (captain) who once served in the Vietnam War, had a degree in Philosophy and Law. This would prove detrimental to every trick in the book that I would try to pull as a teen. He was always a step ahead of me! He was a very strict man, but a man of wisdom and great integrity, stern and to the point. I remember not being able to go to the mall with my girlfriends unless I was purchasing something, not being allowed to put on perfume or anything that in the least bit attracted the opposite sex. You see, we lived in a small town called Gurnee, in which He was an Alderman. This small town also had a naval base located there called Great Lakes which I had a tendency to befriend the sailors, feel sorry for them, and bring them plates of home cooked food from our house. Boy, I'm going to get it when they read this book! I would take them the plates, then run as fast as I could home to try and beat the sun down because I definitely could not be out passed that! My father doesn't remember this next story, but I *most certainly do*! There was a time I had a day off of work and decided to tell him I was going in. However, I worked at Great America and I just wanted to hang out, with my boyfriend that is…Oh, I'm really going to get it now!

My job, in the meantime, called my home and said, "We are a little busier than we thought we'd be. We are going to need Jasmine to come in after all." Oh my goodness! Can you say *bells* and *whistles*? Can you see and hear them going off right now! Upon my return home, I had my gentleman friend drop me off. But my dad, *butcher knife* in hand due to the fact that he was probably cooking, a good cook he was, was waiting in front of the house for me. I almost lost a leg that day! Not by my dad, but by my boyfriend, as he took off before I could get my entire body out of the car! I wonder if He remembers this one Shaun Taylor. Oh, the stories I could tell you. I'm quite sure you have a plethora of your own. Aside from all of that, my dad had a heart of gold. It was a heart that would be broken: shared by a divorce from my mother that would split the two of us for years … until this next moment. I can still remember him standing at the gate of my elementary school watching me play as the separation created tension between the two and caused me at times to not see him. The schoolyard was his best bet at the time of seeing his little girl. He lived on one side of my elementary school and my mom on the other.

I don't know the full story and don't know that I ever will. All I can remember were discussions of child support, paid or not, receipts of proof of pay, and a longing to see him, and to actually live like some of my other friends I knew who were in two parent households. But because I had one parent in the home, I'd often have to stay with a babysitter right in between the two of them, who would often have seizures. It was frightening, to say the least, to see someone have seizures, as some of you may have experienced. It was even more frightening to witness someone lose total control of their body on a regular basis when you are in their care. Oh, how I longed for normalcy, whatever that was. I am still seeking it.

My dad remarried when I was not yet two. This union brought forth a son, my brother and a daughter, my sister, seven and ten years under myself. I recall a conversation with my dad when I was four that I'd never forget as he tried to share with me all about what was going on between he and my mom. He told me that he loved me and that we'd be together again . . . Again, would take place now, living here in Illinois after relocating his family from California due to his job. He worked hard all the time to ensure the financial quality of life he provided for the family. This was a tad different from the day to day struggle experienced in California. It was as though I was in a fantasy land. I lived a pretend life as though it had always been this way. I was so proud. I called my step mom "Mom" in front of people, wanting them to believe my life was not only normal but perfect. It was far from either of those terms. As you can imagine, a teenager coming into anyone's life overnight is not always the business, especially when they are from the former mate.

I was now 15, and looked every bit of the spitting image of the beautiful bride my dad first married. 5 years more and I would have been the age of my mother when she first married at 20. As a kid, I didn't take any of that into consideration. Looking back, I can relate a little bit better since my relationship with my step mom has improved over time, as we have now built our own relationship honoring and acknowledging one another as women, mothers' and most of all children of the most high.

The fairy tale ended quickly. There was a clear and evident split between our extended family blend. The tension was so thick that it could be felt in the air. As much as I desired to fit in and pretend I came from their union like my brother and sister, I didn't. The road I had in mind and the one they had for me did not quite align either. I had been introduced to my high school counselor, who upon meeting and hearing of my interest in cheerleading, as I was the captain of my cheerleading squad back in Oakland at my junior high school, told me that he was also the head girls' basketball coach. He said I should come out because it would be a way that I could meet new friends. Knowing absolutely no one my age in Illinois, I figured that this would be a great idea. His ploy worked… lol. After playing for him awhile, he informed me that this sport would cover my college career if I stayed focused, worked hard and applied myself.

He was right, however, it would be a struggle to obtain due to not having steady transportation to and from practice, as my dad was at work during this time. I fought tooth and nail for the opportunity to play. This was probably the one thing that kept me sane. My coach immediately took me under his wing and saw fit that I'd have a ride to and from practice daily. He also talked with my dad about the potential that I had to further my career. Fortunately, dad, being a ball player himself for Berkley High School and St. Mary's College, understood. He, too, had a passion for the game. With that, I began my basketball career! I began to live in a world that caused me to struggle in not only finding, but also balancing, my identity. I moved from Oakland, California, with a single mom who, at times, had to substitute powdered milk and water for whole milk when it ran out. We'd often roll in our 1972 Ford Bug that my mom still has by the way, to now attending a school in the suburban area of Illinois where my father was the Alderman and I was being dropped off curbside in a Mercedes Benz. This was a culture shock for me as I had become accustomed to taking the A.C. Transit Bus in Oakland to school where there was a liquor store on many a corner and counter built you could often find a church. The students were, for the most part, of African-American descent. My new school was newly built down the road from the amusement park, "Great America" in which I worked in the summer months. It was predominately of a Caucasian decent.

I was one of only a handful of black students in my class. A couple of them were mixed black and white. Some of the classmates who I remember were Corey, Qasim, Robert, Ken, Robee, Ian, Hombre, Cassandra, Nikki, Julie, NaTasha, LaMetra and Clarence, my high school sweetheart, who I was not supposed to have because he was a senior and I a sophomore.:

This of course is minus a couple of names I'm sure to have missed of whom made up our little crew of children of color. I really could literally count them on my hands, as their names are forever engraved in my memory bank and heart. My world was no longer the same. I lived in a shell, a bubble, making my future attempts to mingle with my own color in college an interesting feat.

When the crushing blow of a heartbreak between me and my first mutual love, Clarence Shells, took place as he graduated and went off to college, I'd begin to date my first boyfriend of the Caucasian persuasion, Kevin. He carried my books and walked me to class. He treated me like a queen. We played basketball together, talked sports and simply clicked. I did not understand how he could like me like he did and I failed to receive the love he was trying to share. Friends, to this day, I often think of what may have been. Each step of my journey, I often wonder what could have been as I often do in most relationships I've ever been in. Now I focus on what will be.

CHAPTER THREE

Skirts, Suits, Heels and Sneakers!

Even through all of the hard work, sweat and tears, I always found a way to get into and entangle myself in matters I just had no business. I was terribly good at the two-life type of lifestyle, continuously hiding things I did not desire the public to know. I came upon a man who introduced me to the lesson of STD's (Sexually Transmitted Diseases). I received a call from him that I had given him something and that I needed to pay for his medication.

Disoriented, I ran to a clinic, where I learned I had indeed acquired a couple of these STD'S.. Interestingly enough, I didn't notice symptoms until he called but, nevertheless, I had contracted two venereal diseases. I snuck to the clinic, received medication and became sick from it. I had to bare through the 7 days of treatment, feeling like I was going to die each time I took the meds. It simply was killing my stomach, a feeling I wouldn't wish on anyone! Thank God for a clean bill of health today!

Between all of my high school memoirs with dad, shopping for female products with me, the birds and the bees embarrassment of a discussion before a dance, being escorted to a date by my father to yet another of my boyfriends' (Michael's) house, ("wearing his football jersey was the highlight of our relationship. To me, it showed ownership...that I belonged; something I've been striving to do for years now...belong,") as my dad sat and visited with his father for the duration of the date. I still shake my head while remembering getting my tail whooped after coming home wearing my boyfriend, Clarence Shell's, letterman jacket and ring prior to him going off to college. I wanted to keep it. It was all I had to hang on to. Dad said, "No!" In my heart I felt like I was dying as it's rare a young person can see beyond what they feel in the moment

I was hardheaded; a risk taker, especially when it came to the opposite sex who caught my attention quite often. It didn't help matters when they were cute, athletic or musically gifted . I couldn't help but notice T'Shaun. He was older than me. He was actually not even in high school, yet would be my date later that year to my high school senior prom. We spent hours together; days together, rain, hail, sleet and snow. He, too, challenged me many a day playing one on one in games of basketball. He was my biggest fan! He believed in me. He truly loved me and I loved him. Looking back, those were some of my most intimate times shared with my truest of loves…playing sports! We just had to be together. I couldn't see living my life without him. Soon, there would be an upset that would tear me apart. I went into a depression few could understand and as helpful as Shaun was through it all, we strayed apart. During one of my basketball games, I experienced my first ACL tear and I had to go through surgery. Not able to play the sport that I loved and that kept me sane through high school crushed me. Thank God I had already signed my scholarship for college. This was an area Shaun just could not comfort me in no matter how hard he tried.

My siblings were right there with me, through the highs and the lows. The heated and the funny! Even though they were a lot younger than me, they were with me through it all! My brother, the little scientist, would lace string through the entire house like the laser security system in the movies *The Matrix* or *Mr. and Mrs. Smith*, so no one could walk up and down the stairs. There were days he'd make concoctions and blow up the kitchen with flour and whatever sodium product he had mixed together with acidic substances.

I just knew I was going to get in trouble due to his unwarranted, self-assigned projects. He was tough to watch but kind and sweet as he could be. Oftentimes, sneaking me cookies downstairs to my room in the basement, saying that he found them and he was aware that I had not had any. Folded in his sweaty little palms were mushed up cookies; for me! Tears flow remembering his acts of kindness and his heart for me.

My little sister is beautiful, tough as nails and sassy as they come. She was the little general who told us all, and is still telling us to this day, how it's all going to go down and exactly how it's going to be! Lol... Loved this kid! She was my heart. I remember talks with her when she was only 5 years old. I'd come into her room and sit on the foot of her bed.

I downloaded to her all that I was going through and, attentively, she would listen; at times even offering advice. A memory that we share and re-tell at all of our family gatherings though too far and few are the times. I would have her to break up with my boyfriends for me over the phone . . . love her for that. I had a personal secretary and dictator. Unbelievable years I tell you. Last, I remember putting her on the little yellow school bus my senior year in high school as she was just beginning her years of elementary schooling and I on to college. Not much has changed except that we're a little older. I was even blessed with the honor of officiating her wedding! We siblings have stuck together fighting against all odds to maintain our unity as one, despite our family blended parenting. Though distant in geography, we were successful in our plight. My children know them as aunt and uncle and that's it. Now, I will soon be an auntie!

Eventually, the pattern had been established that when things get rough, you bail or escape. I had not acquired the skills to problem solve and had learned that my audience had a deaf ear to it anyway, so with that fight or flight mindset of mine, I *flew*! Yes, I had run away again. I had my share of high school boyfriends and more inappropriate dealings… It never stopped. Not sure who'd ever want me as a wife at this point. Nothing was reserved or special anymore as I had begun to misuse and abuse my body quite often. I'd stay at my friend's house whose parents were subsequently friends of my dad's and step mom's, and that, too, put a strain on their relationship.

I felt I was the cause of not much good. There I'd stay the remainder of my senior year until I graduated from high school. More cake, hugs and fake smiles were shared. Again, somehow I maintained decent grades, went down state to compete and represent my school's choral program, singing *Sometimes I Feel like a Motherless Child.* I was one of the top basketball players in my area, the top player at my school and only female ball player to receive a full-ride basketball scholarship to college from my high school at that time. A gift sent straight from God. This is where my independence would begin. This is where I'd find myself, I thought. I could only hope I wasn't already too lost.

Submerged with anger, resentment and self-afflicted abuse, I trudged on to school. Sigh… Life could now begin. Not realizing it had already begun and I was just now at the first quarter. I hadn't even made it to half time! With no adult supervision and away from military house rules of tucking your bed in the corners, you can only imagine what could, would and did take place. Feeling rejected, unfulfilled, tired, desperate for attention and love, the only thing I needed to hear was *I Love You*, and you could have from me just about anything you wanted. I can't tell you how many times I was in love. I didn't stay in a relationship. I didn't say that they loved me, liked me or get this, even knew me. I was in love, at each encounter. I was also in agony every two weeks when the other girls were in love too…*with the same guy or guys even*!

I was officially sick to my stomach and nauseous at the idea that not one of my fairytale relationships had come true.

Fairytale

I often wonder how the story really ends

 after life's stent of twists, turns and bends

 Does the light truly exist at the end of the tunnel

 Is there really a rainbow a pot of gold sits under

 Will the boogie man get me if I fall off to sleep

Will I drowned in my tears when the water gets deep

Can Superman save me from that deep blue sea

"Float like a butterfly sting like a bee"

What magnificent gifts has God given thee?

But will I live like Job to even see...

The generations of fruit that will follow me

If I wish on a star and click my heals three times

Will the clock strike midnight will the bell tower chime

Fairy God mother's calling telling me it's time

Stop running with the mice tic toc tic toc

up and down that brown little clock

You were born to fly wonder woman up high

Avenging as you sail through the sky

I'm gonna get there where the skies are blue

Don't wanna be stuck old lady in the shoe

For if I do...I just might crack.....

 See Humpty Dumpty sat on that wall

but the kings men and horses won't let me fall

Down that hole like Alice and Rabbit

I was born to l fly I'll just reach up and grab it

Alladin's Carpet of course, Take Jasmine's hand

Hi Peter! Hi Wendy! I pray to Never land

Cinderella Cinderella come fly with me

The skies are blue and my soul is free

Many lessons are learned as stories unfold

Thank God for the scribe thank God they were told...

The three little bears learned life's not fair
Little Red Riding hood learned to conquered her fear
Snow White will never again eat from strangers
The Gingerbread man learned to run from danger
Beauty and the Beast taught to love from inside
Pinocchio paid each time that he lied
Lil Bo peep will tend better to his sheep
Dorothy...ariel, rapunzel
And in the end we still may not know
It's in our hearts innocence we keep
It's in our dreams that we'll find sweet sleep
Until then I'll wait on that kiss
Not from the frog but from my handsome prince!
Now to create our own fairytales and laughter
In the moonlight we'll Happily ever after

I ran back to California, on a plane, that is! Can you guess where? Yes, to my first love, my first experience. I ran to Charles. I went to his college campus, where he played on the football team. I was back to my comfort zone. I was going to drop out of school and stay with him forever. I was a freshman in college at this point. We dreamt of a life together. We spoke of a house we'd buy and the trophy room we'd have of all of our accomplishments. That's what I adored about him. He allowed me to dream. Little did I know, he, too, had gotten into a relationship that, though it was not going so well, did produce fruit, in fact that very night. There I was rushing to the hospital with him where I stayed, in the car, that is, until his baby was born.

Years later, I'd see that many of the events in my life appeared to be cyclical due to not dealing with the root of issues each situation stemmed from. Each of the situations had common roots, soiled and potted the same and producing similar fruit each time. He did not allow me to stay, knowing this would interfere with my future. He made me go back to school. He said he could not live with the fact of me possibly not succeeding because of him. He had already been blamed for so much dating back to our childhood years. Head low and heart broken, I went back to school.

I wanted to go home! I couldn't make it here in college, so I felt. I asked to come home and was told my room had been turned into an office. I was crushed. I called a girlfriend of mine from my high school. She said I could come and stay with her and her roommates. Although I was in college, I was made to feel that I was a big old kid. Really, I was. I was taken care of by the University and women's basketball program, who paid my way through school, purchased and retrieved my books for me, set up my dorm arrangements, scheduled all of my classes, and fed me well. I was blessed, but pretty much sheltered, and crippled, flat out spoiled! I didn't know how to do anything on my own, including renting an apartment, cooking, paying bills or anything domestic.

All the things one must do in the real world, I didn't have a clue of. I couldn't drive nor did I have a driver's license. I became a weight and burden to my friends. They all had jobs and were pulling their own weight. They were in skirts, suits and heels. I was in a sweat suit with sneakers and a ball cap. The young adult crew that let me stay with them that summer and I were clearly in two different worlds. I couldn't help to feel many of them were a tad jealous of the athlete status and all that came with it, because many of them could not afford to go off to college and had to work to earn an earnest living. Truth be told, neither could I. I was simply blessed with favor produced by my early on hard work through my gift of playing ball. They took on early adult roles, working, driving, managing money and having babies. They were mini adults. I, clearly still a big child and they made me feel it. I was struggling real hard to find myself. I was torn between many worlds and many identities.

I did what any big kid would do. I called my mother. She used her connections to gain me an internship for the summer because I had nowhere to go. I had to grow up, or continue living at the least. I moved to Texas for the summer to take on an internship at an oil company under a man my mom used to work for back in the day. He was a man of power with lots of money. This would be good for me. I had to work to earn my own living, wear those fancy clothes and shoes my friends were wearing, show up on time, make my own play money and get this, pay my own rent. It didn't take long at all and I was already attached. Believe that one? Of course you do. There was no secret to my dysfunctional pattern whatsoever.

I had a new boyfriend who lived with his mom, no pattern adjustment there either but of course in this case we were kids and again who was I to judge I was just blessed to have had the opportunity to play college ball on full scholarship. I was in another state and completely free! Pastor Wiley once reminded me of this next saying some time ago when I was in my early 20's "When you go on vacation, God goes too! It's not like you leave Him behind and He can't catch up with you till' you get back. Ha! I had apparently not grasped that concept just yet. You see, I was on vacation! I did whatever, whenever and however I could possibly do it. Clearly, I was out of my league and Texas got the best of this little girl. Can you say turn out? My Lord! What an experience. What's the saying? What happens' in Vegas stays in Vegas? Only my Vegas, was Houston, Texas!

I survived, barely, hitting the clubs until I couldn't see straight and bringing all sorts of people home. The likes didn't matter~even acquaintances and/or associates of my boyfriend,

Byron, including his family and some of their friends. I didn't know many of these people well, but they'd all come back to my pad on occasion to conclude the after party. Still stuck on my first love, my Houston boyfriend caught wind that I had communicated with my California first love and dumped me. I was hurt, alone and in another State. Summer turned cold real fast and would come to an abrupt end to what felt like years. I went back to school in the fall a wreck. I hadn't trained the first. I was an emotional wreck and no one could relate because they weren't in Never-Never-Land with me to experience the things I had just experienced. It was up to me to get me out of this rut. Now just how was I going to do that?

I began to reach out to the world and off campus to find my ground, over a place to belong, or a person to love me. First, to a boyfriend whom the men's basketball team gave me much slack about because, yes, he was white and I was actually leaving the dorm to go and live with him. These were my so called big brothers that liked me behind closed doors, if you know what I mean, but called me little sister in public because I was a tom boy and not sexy like the groupie girls as I called them that would come to their basketball games dressed in high heels and wearing lipstick. I didn't attract them in that way. However, when I decided to move off campus with my boyfriend, who played on the men's baseball team, that deemed to be a problem for them.

That relationship that everyone thought would last a lifetime, did not. He had plans of going to play professional ball as many scouts were looking at him. Because of this, he felt the seeds planted in our union would not be wise to water or harvest due to the outcome it could have on his potential future career. I was devastated to say the least. Can't say exactly the cause of our separation, as our families were already intermingled, my folks with his, if you get my drift. We were the ideal couple, match made in heaven. Somewhere in there, I wanted to find out what life was like on the outside of college before making that plunge, even though he had it all figured out. You see, if he did not make it to the pro's, he was going to be a Doctor and then He would pay my way through school and I could be his assistant. I, on the other hand, didn't see it quite that way. I wanted to know what I could become with or without a man. Sure enough, he became a Chiropractic Doctor and I, still without a man. I don't know if I struggle more with the fact that he became successful like he said he would, without me, as I struggle day to day trying to provide for my children whose fathers are not in the home, or with the fact that he eventually married and had children that I had to give up. I suppressed the emotional trauma of the loss in order to survive. It's not something I deal with often due to the magnitude of pain that is associated with it. Needless to say, Facebook is hard to watch when scrolling through the milestones of their offspring and wives or chosen girlfriends. I don't know exactly how this life works, for I have two of the most outstanding children in the world and truth be told, right or wrong, they could not have been born had my others made it through. Still, to this day, I try to process the loss of life that once lived inside me. I'm sure somewhere in his heart he must too.

I sat in the waiting room of a Planned Parenthood facility…becoming too familiar with the looks of hopelessness, despair and out right gloom of the faces that surrounded me. While I waited my turn, stomach in knots tighter than the thoughts twisted in my mind…alone, again, I looked overhead. There was posted a television set. The only thing that kept my mind off of the horrific events to follow was watching a white truck being broadcast just driving and driving… This seemed to go on forever as I watched in a transfixed state of mind. I realized at that moment that somewhere, somebody was also going through life changing events. Truly, I was not alone. It was O.J. Simpson on the day of the big chase prior to his arrest of the alleged murder of Nicole. In my mind, my ordeal was the biggest thing ever and to me, it was. However, O.J., the milk man, the grocer at the store, the hairstylist down the street, the lawyer, the doctor, the school teacher and yes, even *you*, I'm sure were also going through something on that day, had just come out of something or would be going through something soon! Mindful, it's not just me in the midst of this big ol' world. I tried to handle my storm as best I could. I walked into the room, cold and sterile. I de-robed and gowned up. Shaking, I lay across the table. I was scared. I was sad. I was so out of the will of God, and so far away from home. I closed my eyes as the cold hands of the doctor clasped my arm in efforts to place the needle that would fill my veins with the anesthesia needed to put me out. I saw a white light overhead, almost blinding. I began to tremble even the more. Tears rolled down the corners of my eyes as I felt them roll into my ears. I began to slowly fade away...maybe....... just maybe.... I would not wake up at all and I could go with my baby and leave this world behind.

Not long, thereafter, I awoke. I was empty, angry, ashamed and lost. Game day was around the corner...One of many. I am exactly three days, post abortion and I can't sit out! I even tried to stay home from practice but was told to be there even if I only sat on the floor to get the plays and hear the instruction. Being sick was *not* an excuse not to play in the world of college basketball... you were a paid commodity you see. Stretch, pop some meds, shoot that knee up, wrap it tight, drink a sip of water, and get back in the game! I'm not lying... ask most athletes that you may know in your neighborhood that ever played on scholarship. We were brought there to get the job done! That was my daily motivation and goal; get the job done! I couldn't risk telling my coaches that I couldn't play due to an abortion. I may lose my scholarship, be sent home and lose face to my community and those rooting and cheering for me to succeed and be that representative I had claimed to be for them. I never considered the representative I was failing to be for God. While I only saw the ball, God saw it all. The grace was definitely uncommon and necessary to the call.

I stood up, wanting to pass out, swallowed, uncovered my hands from my face, looking up to God and breathing deeply. I could hear the loud music piping from the stadium speakers, the crowd a blur, my teammates expecting me to be on point! Feet were pounding in the bleachers' along with the loud chants of "Let's go ladies let's go . . . *clap, clap, stomp, stomp!* I squeezed my eyes tight leaving only enough room split between my eyelash (less) eyelids to see the University emblem on the center of the gym floor and the shoelaces of my non-starting teammates and mascot that had lined up to slap us five prior to us running out into the game. The announcer proceeded with the starting line-up. My name was called. A bright light flashed! Leaving behind yet another child I will never know; I entered the game. Now I see exactly where the phrase "Game Face" comes from. For this is the way I have lived my entire life. This is the way many live their lives to this day. Show no weakness! Show no Pain! Deliver! Deliver strong and don't complain! There's no invitation to celebrate your glory. No one needs to know your pity-party story! What a trick of the enemy!

This served me well in the game of basketball, but crippled me in the game of life. I've needed help in this world. I've needed a lot of help! However, this being my mindset of what mental and physical toughness looked like, I failed to be transparent in areas that would have allowed me access to the help I really needed, what I am just now learning to receive and retrieve in order to help another.

Sometimes, we get so deep into our sin that climbing out seems impossible. We try to cover it up in hopes that it will disappear or just go away. But guess what? It doesn't without the help of God. It is something you will carry a lifetime if you don't learn to give it over to Him. Learning to face it becomes crucial. We must acknowledge it, learn from it, repent and begin to seek ways of help and move forward. God is our help. He is our refuge. He is our way out! He will give us the strength to carry on, and the courage to stand bold and represent His name. We now have a story to tell and a responsibility to reach out and help each other.

CHAPTER FOUR

Taking it to My Grave!

After moving from the apartment, comfort and protection with my boyfriend, I'd then turn to the wolves. Out in the world and alone where the professional athletes would eat me alive. I thought I had a handle on things; I did not. Waking up in ball player after ball players' rooms as they'd come into town, flattering me and showering me with praise, not even gifts, just words, became my way of living for a while. Jesus!

There'd be times they'd invite their friends in to brag, or observe with the expectation of joining in. They'd begin to fight over me as if I was an object and not a person, arguing for a turn...wait...what???, That's when enough was enough. I don't really care to go into details, as it is all really ugly enough. I concluded, at that time, that I was not anyone's trophy piece or a play toy! I couldn't stand what was becoming of me. I couldn't stand the thought of what I'd come to find out later, that my baby sister and I both had encounters with one of the same guys. As if the world wasn't big enough. Could I have my own? I couldn't even have my own mess-ups, short-comings or downfalls, I thought to myself. I needed so badly to have ownership over something, anything. I didn't want to feel anymore.

I needed to numb myself so I didn't have to face the reality of things I had done and experienced. Things I could not take back. Just looking at myself disgusted me. I was constantly feeling as though my reputation was slipping little by little and would be gone totally if I did not get things under control. Fortunately, the individuals I was dealing with were on the outside, but my world was growing smaller as the professional athlete circle was not that large. I did not want to become labeled as . . . well, anything but wife material. What I was definitely not preparing for at the time.

Smoking was never my thing, seeing as though I was an athlete and all, but something had to be done to cloud the picture because I was beginning to see things for what they were. So, I starting drinking. Beer was the cheapest thing I could find at the time on a college student budget. I would drink until I couldn't feel any more. There were times it was so bad that you could still smell the alcohol coming from my pours at basketball practice the next day. I began to miss classes, sleeping all day, before my coach intervened and began checking our classes to see if we were there or not and making it mandatory that we sat in the front three rows of classes that were at times 300 people deep or more. One night I went to the store and bought a jug of Monte Carlos Rossi. You could get those for a couple of bucks. I took it back to my dorm room, sat on my top bunk bed and drank until it was gone. I felt as if angels watched overhead as I passed out.

I was pulled out of my bed, fortunately, by one of the basketball players from the men's team… He lifted me from the throw up that I was surrounded in. Blessed I was, as that alone, throwing up in my sleep, could have caused me to choke to death. Glory be unto God. I am here to either write about it and help someone else or look good while taking it to my grave.

What benefit is it to gain the world and to lose your soul. My soul or anyone else's for that matter. Mathew 16:26/ Mark 8:36 Later that week, I was in the hospital there on my school's campus. We were a medical school you see. In fact, later in life, I delivered my daughter there. The nurses and doctors still remembered me! However, this trip proved to be not as nice. I would be there in and out the next four weeks as I bled for approximately 28 days. This, would in turn carry into and/or from a miscarriage I'd have with one of my ball player boyfriends on campus. Truthfully, he was hurt. He showed affection and remorse, which was more love than I had felt in a long time, whether it was for me or the loss I received it. I suited up and carried on. I was paid for as an athlete and game day was always around the corner. This was what I had come here for. Right? Oh and an education to secure my future was sure to be in there somewhere.

I would awake one day to a message from the front desk at the dorm stating that I had received flowers! I thought to myself, finally a glimpse of light. Someone cared. Only that someone was a *girl*! Ok, can it get worse? Initially, I was so offended, appalled, embarrassed, and let down. However, I was at this moment, now turned on to the world of lesbianism. I was looking in whatever direction I could look to find love, be loved, desired or just to be. This was my outlet. I thought to myself, nothing else seemed to be working and this would be a way that a man could never hurt me again! I just wouldn't deal with them at all.

I found myself in an entire other arena. I would soon have myself a girlfriend. I don't remember her name. I do remember she was pretty. This was my opportunity to take the dominant stance and play the male role for a change. I had a chance to finally be in that man's role and not what I considered the weaker submitted role in that of a woman. I could control or dictate the outcome of the relationship now, or so I thought. No one was going to hurt or leave me ever again. I wasn't born or raised this way, in fact this was extremely foreign to me. However, I was just trying to find myself; trying to survive, live and not die, as I felt my soul being consumed daily until the point would come that I'd seek alternative means of not being here at all. The inability to be loved is devastating. I had not learned yet the concept of first loving yourself. So, I was already fighting an uphill battle. Eventually, being that this was not a natural thing for me. The girlfriend thing didn't pan out too well. I'd fail at that, too. I had been with everybody from the security guard on our campus who I truly bonded with and found great friendship in, even to this day, to the recruits coming in to sign and now, this girl! I'd end up working in a massage parlor for extra money. Seeing as though, at the time, it was a violation to be employed under NCAA rules and regulations for fully signed scholarship athletes, I would take this up during a summer month to keep me afloat.

Throughout the semesters, I received financial aid checks that I would frivolously blow from 19 through 22 years of age. I never had to budget anything as an athlete that was fully taken care of. The money was good, and I was spoiled. I was not having sex for this money. The addiction was that I could get it just for them looking at me while they received full body massages. I wasn't even mature enough, knowledge wise, to perform some of the requested acts they had for me to do, so they would do it themselves, while staring at me in a bikini covering a body I'd give almost anything to have again.

That alone was enough to make your stomach turn; some of these men being 70 plus years old with tons of money and nothing better to spend it on, not even their wives. Now that was a mouthful. Talk about selling my soul to the devil. Again I asked myself could this get any worse?

Nothing but God kept me. I've come to learn that one of the women who trained me died of aids in there, after performing acts that got her paid a lot more money than I. She was the owner's wife and madam of the house. She was beautiful, with a body to die for, sweet and had a life that, from the outside, appeared ever so glamorous. I think of countless days that I was so close to taking that next step, allowing men to use my body and being able to financially do and have whatever I wanted; everything but peace, everything but *my life*. It was nothing but the remembrance of the Word of God that got me out of there. Many a day, we were raided; just so happens, it was on days when I was off. No records were found of me, because we all had aliases. It's all like a bad dream to me now, a memory that can't seem to erase out of my head, no matter how many praise and worship songs I sing, but for the Word of God that permeates my soul and says…

He will not always accuse, nor will he harbor his anger forever; he does not treat us as our sins deserve or repay us according to our iniquities. For as high as the heavens are above the earth, so great is his love for those who fear him; as far as the east is from the west, so far has he removed our transgressions from us. Psalm 103:9-12

Well, I plan on giving the enemy as less attention as possible in this book, so bottom line is: two abortions, a miscarriage, and a side job at the local massage parlor that would support my extra financial needs through college. Later, I'd find myself graduated as one of the University's top players in history holding record stats for rebounds, blocked shots, field goal percentage and even scoring until the generation knocked me out of the scoring bracket. I was only a couple hundred points shy of my 1000-point mark. Who knows what other records I could have set, if I had not torn my ACL. I also received a leadership award from the Alumni Association at a year-end banquette.

See, I told you somehow I was able to mess up so badly, time after time, cover it up and still come out on top. In the world's eyes that is, but God knew better.

Pretty Face

Used and abused in this race running
With no direction til' the pain
I faced is all erased but never the less
I can't keep up with the pace of this road I'm goin' down

Quickly I fall, hit the ground rollin'
Oh No! Here they come patrolln'
Has it all been a waste?
His life I've disgraced?
No! It's Not Over!
I pull out my mace n' spray into the face
Of the devil who's laced

My life with lies and deceit!
No longer will I receive the news of defeat!
That's not for me!
That's not my case!
There's so much more behind this pretty face

As interesting as it all was, I am grateful for the game of basketball and a father, coaches and an uncle who saw my potential in it. They believed in me and pushed me to excel. Because of it, I believe I was able to maintain my sanity. It was one thing that gave me a sense of belonging. The game was a vehicle where I could gain respect, be looked up to and needed.

It was one area where I actually felt people competing for me! I was wined and dined paraded and adorned, something I had not felt up until that point or ever again necessarily. Until, I accepted Jesus and learned of His fine style in living and lavish spread of food that would enrich my life forever.

Graduation Day…and mixed emotions. You can only imagine what I'm feeling by this time. Oh did I say more cake, hugs and now fear of the unknown. I had already established a victim mindset and feared the next predator, never realizing I had any form of control over my situation. Again, the Lord who has been with me the entire time, blesses me with a job to take care of myself. That has to be one of the saving graces in my life. I have always been able to support myself. I have always encountered the most awesome experiences by way of my education, travel, or jobs and even through my children. God knows what we can bare and sets us up perfectly like the volleyball setter for a perfect score! Favor was upon me. It felt like things were handed to me on a silver platter at this point. I was happy. Possibly, I could put this behind me and find that perfect life I was searching for.

I became a women's basketball coach, beginning my career at Loyola University. It wouldn't be long before my assistant title would change to head coach. Midway through the season, our head coach left! Talk about growing up. There was no time to cry, panic or be afraid. I learned to take the bull by the horns and steer. I have been that way ever since. I was now an interim head coach at 24 years of age. In fact, I was the youngest head coach in the NCAA Mid-West Collegiate Conference. Though, at the time, I didn't think much of it. Like Adam in the garden, what a privilege it was to be there and in relational positioning. However, I was too naive to understand the magnitude of it all. I never fully walked into position. I couldn't see or receive my worth. I never took over the physical office of my former head coach, as I, again, didn't deem myself worthy. I remained in my little assistant coach office as not to upset my other co-workers who were not chosen for the position. There are things in this lifetime that you will be graced with and shown great favor. We must learn to receive gifts when they are given and walk into position held high like the kings and queens we were called to be. Of course, I had not yet acquired this mindset. I was looking to please man and not God something many of us do. He has been trying to elevate me my entire life and I continually sabotage the plan by not accepting and walking into the gift.

What a shame and how costly this was. To think of how things could have really been. I often wonder how far along I could've been by now. Anywho, as my grandmother used to say, this brought with it some challenges, as you can imagine. I'm sure co-workers wondered why me and not them. Possibly thinking that they had put in the more time and were more skilled at the game. But favor is something to be reckoned with. It strained relationships that, to this day, are iffy and prayerfully fixable.

We will all have our challenges and pick our sin of choice, if it doesn't pick us first. By now, I'm sure you know the area in which mine resided. It didn't help much that I had just graduated from college myself a year prior and the students and players weren't but a year to three younger than I. Thursday night was the big party night. I had to watch all of the young people my age, walk past my apartment to the bars, while I stayed indoors pouting. I was now *Coach* grown enough to have my own job and apartment but immature still in a sense that I didn't even have my own driving license or car. I would foot it, take the "L" short for the subway system we had in Chicago or bus or jump into someone else's vehicle. My dad said, "Oh No!" You're in college. I'm not getting your license so you can go off to college driving everyone around on my insurance! He wanted his baby girl to have a life! So, I didn't get one until my college boyfriend refreshed my dad and mom's early on training, allowing me to use his car after graduation to finally become licensed.

There's a certain respect and prestige that comes with being the *Coach* but also a responsibility that is out of this world. What happens now in the area of dating??? All of the guys on the men's team were my age too! Perplexed was not even the word. One of the guys I dated in college was actually on the men's team there but had graduated that year as well. Whew! I skated by without any major trauma and was fortunate enough to meet gentlemen off campus which led to abortion number... Eventually, I would meet the father of my first born child.

CHAPTER FIVE

Invincible

It would be a night out in Chicago that I spent, as I was now an adult. I was a very young adult, but nevertheless an adult. I've always sang, be it in church, school, family functions or yes, even in the nightclubs. This particular night, I was singing at a club that later would burn down taking the lives of several young people, even a couple of friends of mine. This particular night, I was singing in the lower portion of the club. This would serve as the classier of the levels. There was a two drink minimum, white cloth dressed tables, with a sort of jazzy feel type of setting. On a break, I went upstairs to the hip-hop club to meet who would eventually be the father of my first born child. Funny story, maybe even red flag, but everything happens for a reason. I paraded back and forth in front of him until he'd eventually take notice of me. We exchanged numbers and I didn't hear from him for close to a month. Now a college coach, with my own office and voicemail, Jimmy would later admit that it was quite intimidating to realize, after hearing my work voicemails, that he had run across a college graduated head coach of a D1 NCAA Women's Basketball team. He said he called a couple of times and hung up! Lol. I felt rejected, feeling he didn't want me, instead of realizing it was just the opposite. He really was interested, but for the status behind my title. We laughed about it later. I didn't think much of it at the time. In fact, I have never thought much of myself nor my accomplishments. I never saw life in status arenas. I considered myself the girl next door and, to this day, I'm sure that is one of the contributing factors to my singleness and lack of elevated status. Thus, the saying you are what you think you are... Yet my humble heart keeps me open to the world at large. I am what many call approachable and easy to talk to. This has been a strength and a fault of mine.

Now, as a mature, spiritually-minded child of God, I can reflect back and see where my road began to bend. He would later admit to me as well that my degree was intimidating and conversations at times amongst my family and friends, he felt left out of or uncomfortable, even though this man was, and is, one of the most intelligent men I know and is knowledgeable in areas I wouldn't dream of researching. Paper is paper.

Credentials are credentials and, honestly, it does separate people. It is what they call *unequally yoked*. No one higher than the other, just not yoked up the same. It causes for tensions, frustrations, and inevitable separation. Background, foundation, goals and beliefs are every bit of important in relationship building. Back to the night of our first encounter, I was flattered by the attention. I thought I had found family. I was getting older and was ready to settle down so I could be protected and hurt no more. I thought he would be this to me and for me. He wasn't. I had already placed a huge weight on him by taking me on period with all of my and internal challenges. I clamped on and gripped strong. He was not ready for that. Although he professed love and the possibility of marriage, the fact that, again, our foundation had nothing to do with God but the lust of the flesh left no room for possible success, yet, the thirst for more flesh.

He had just lost his brother and I was now pregnant without the assured promise of anything. Get this, not one but two emotional wrecks. Throughout my pregnancy, I even wore a bubble gum machine ring to church (Rock of Ages Baptist Church, where I had begun attending in hopes of a chance of healing. I didn't want my fantasy bubble to burst! I wanted to be accepted by the people of God.) I sat in the balcony of our two-story church desperately trying to hide my belly and waiting to deliver, so I could get back up there in the choir stand.

My start of yet another fantasy of a relationship crashed and burned at the very beginning. He would be expecting another child shortly thereafter and the realization that what I thought was mine was not, "again" slapped me in the face. We went to the hospital with my first born, Lyric, to welcome the new baby. The doctor told me I had to wait in the waiting room because I was not family.

The sickest feeling came over me. Sicker than the day I found out his side relationship had even existed . . . *light bulb moment!* "You are not married Jasmine and this is not your husband despite the fact that you live as though you are." I was reminded of that very fact by my friend, Niki. I was a baby mama! What? The audacity! That is not me! I am wife material! I am not a baby mama!

The very thought began to kill my soul even more than it had already been killed. This could not be happening. So I went into attack mode. Only, I attacked myself, unfortunately. I wanted him to love me, to desire me more than her. So, I did everything but the right thing. I began to stop eating. I took weight loss pills, and green teas and whatever else I could get my hands on to look good on the outside, even though I was messed up on the inside. Eventually my body gave way, and I passed out. My daughter, now approaching two, was walking on me as I lay on the floor lifeless. I can't recall if I heard the phone or not, nor how his mom came in to find me, but she took me to the hospital where they immediately placed in me an I.V. to bring my vitals back up. The doctor said had I not made it there, I may not be here at all. My chance of a normal life gone over night! We tried to continue our relationship and make it work, but it didn't.

What happens now? What package do I have to offer now? I was already wounded but nobody could see it. I have a radiant smile, so I've been told, though it didn't portray the things I had been through. More shame and embarrassment began to come to the surface through my actions. Who's going to want me with a kid? How am I going to make it now? They will think I am not worth it. If he cheated on me, I must be no good. I placed my worth in his hands instead of the Master's, not realizing this man had been operating in pain too.

To this day, we are the best of friends, which is truly a blessing, realizing we were both kids at the time. We raise our daughter together even from a distance, we do the best we can. It didn't change the fact that I self-medicated with men, like I did best, to find more hurt and more of my soul being sucked out with each sexual encounter I'd have. When would it end? I did find comfort in a certain man, but due to complicated connections, we deemed it impossible to ever have a relationship that anyone would understand or approve of. Fond memories we will always share, working out and spending the quality time I could, otherwise, not spend with anyone else. I am comforted now knowing he, too, has found the Lord and saved a place for me in his heart as well.

I had begun to reach out to the Lord for myself, like my former Minister of Music, Smokey Norful's song says, "not a second or another minute, not an hour or another day." I had given my life back over to the Lord. I was smart enough to realize He was the only way I would ever be able to get myself out of this mess I had created and begin to find any kind of peace.

I picked myself up by the bootstraps and applied to grad school. I'd always had this invincible attitude about life and the things I could do. I was what they called a jack of all trades; master of none. I'd jump from one thing to the next and actually excel at it. I became a part-time police officer and taught school, all while playing in the Pro-Am and mothering a newborn.

Out of the 400 individuals that tried out for the police academy, 200 of us passed the first bout of writing tests. Another 100 would be cut due to not passing the physical exam, which included jumping 6 feet walls, pulling 100 lb. plus dummies up and through a window to safety, and amongst other things, running a mile and a half in a timed limit. Out of 100 prospects remaining, I made the list!

After some took other job positions, I ended up #2 on the list. I became the vice president of my police academy class and received the Leadership award presented to me by our town's mayor. Although my police department co-workers rallied behind and around me, unfortunately, this was not favored by many of my male counterparts in other precincts. To me, it was natural. It was just who I was, how I was designed, what I did and simply the cloth I was cut from. My daughter's father and I tried but didn't make it through many attempts to remain together. With that said, hard times began to present themselves in my young adult life. Because of my undergraduate collegiate career, I had options to return to school for my masters. I entered graduate school in the fall and became the hall resident advisor so that my housing would be free. I worked part-time for the men's basketball team in ticket sales so that my tuition would be covered. I enrolled my daughter into the pre-school on campus and kept it stepping. I was desperate for a new life, a new start. I enrolled in everything I couldn't do in under grad due to my rigorous basketball schedule. These were my original passions, like keyboarding (piano), chamber choir, and *writing*.

I was a writing consultant on campus for writers that needed help with their writing skills and/or simple editing and arranging. Go figure! I did not see this book coming *at all*. I, as well, took up theatre and performed in plays. Here I was able to practice my public speaking from undergraduate work in the media sports program at our school, announcing live hockey games to improvisational acting, which was my favorite, of course, as it was yet another way to escape from the real world that was at hand. Talk about a busy schedule . . . This is what I did. Drop one thing and overload on another so that I'd have zero time to think and zero time to live. I was *exhausted!* I was much too busy to be sad or depressed. I could only do this for so long. I ran from my past situation but not so far that he, my daughter's father, couldn't reach us, as my college was all of 20 minutes outside of the town where I was living.

This was in hopes that he'd come back for us, but that didn't ever happen. There were times my baby would get all dressed up, suitcase in hand, waiting at the front door and then receive news her daddy would not be able to make it on that night but perhaps another. She'd be devastated and I, heartbroken for her, as there was nothing I could do to comfort her pain. The feeling of watching her hurt was agonizing for me and almost unbearable, but as a mother, it was my responsibility to console her the best I could. I needed to be her rock and her constant. I tried. To this day, I am still trying.

She was, and still is, daddy's little girl. She'd refuse to take her clothing off in hopes that he would still come and would eventually fall asleep fully clothed. Between the mental and physical exhaustion, I'd found hope and another chance at love. I'd give my all to a man named Marquis. I gave him every part of me, including my heart, because I just knew he was the one for me. Smart, handsome, great with my daughter and I do believe he loved me!

My schedule consisted of finishing an overnight shift as dorm residence advisor, dropping my preschooler to school heading to work with the men's basketball department, then off to class, over to the gym for a couple of pickup games, back to pick up my daughter from preschool, off to chamber choir and gospel choir rehearsals, and back home to try and complete grad school homework with a crying 2-3-year-old, then back to my dorm resident duties. I'd eventually run out of steam.

I had decided there was no purpose for me to be here any longer, struggling alone with no hope any longer of ever rekindling with her father and no real assurance that a relationship with him would best prosper in this manner. I felt they'd have a better opportunity of a relationship if I went back home to California and sent her to spend time with him without me. She has done this now since age 6, as I traveled with her the first two years. I left even with the heart tugging pull of a young gentleman I had just met and to this day feel could have finally been the one; amongst all of the other one's right? I was so confused. I reconnected with mom, who said to come home, as she would help me with the baby, something that she could fully relate to. Shortly thereafter, I was on a plane to California with my 3-year-old daughter; 16 years of my life had flashed before my eyes. Like a time-warp, I was back home.

CHAPTER SIX

Kicking Motion

Now, back in California, I had moved to my own duplex after a few months of living with my mother. Things all of a sudden got real. For the first time, I experienced a crossover into adulthood. I was scared. Both of my parents, at separate times, in transitional points in their lives had to come stay with lil ol' me. I realized I could no longer lean on them, for in this season, I would be the shoulder. I had to quickly try to solidify myself financially because there was now no one to turn to for help. This season, like all, came and went with its own stresses, trials and tribulations. I began yet another unhealthy relationship. I didn't say unwanted. I said it was unhealthy. It would be with a man named Ryan, a college graduated athlete, football player to be exact. Yes, I wanted to marry him too. In the end… I, again, had to accept that I was not the chosen one. When our relationship didn't work out, I medicated with whom today would be known as my son's father, a 19, going on 20-year-old, college football player. I, by this time, was 30 going on 31. I know, I know, *How Stella Got Her Groove Back* take two. Book over! Not even close, just beginning. What had I done? This, a to-be-behind-closed-doors relationship, came as close to the light as going home to be with Jesus or so it felt. To make matters worse, it was a former student of my mother's and if pride wasn't already a factor, … The pain continued as, of course, his advice to me was to go to the abortion clinic. For me, this presented a flashback to a former chapter in my life that I swore I would never revisit In agony, realizing not only was this his request but, he didn't want me, and he sure didn't want our baby. Angrily, I went. However, unclothed and all, laying on the table, the nurse came in. Papers signed and all, the only thing needed to get started was the injection of anesthetic.

However, she said, "I took a picture. Would you like to see it?" I couldn't help but to say yes. I looked and beheld my child in my womb. So precious was the sign of two arms, two legs, and all bodily functions alive and in kicking motion. I cried, got up from the table and walked out! No more. *The abortions end here and today*! I got to a point where I just didn't care anymore. It was easier that way... Living reckless...will never happen for me again!

If Tears Could Talk

If tears could talk, what would they say?
Running downhill they'd try to scamper away;
Wish I could go, go far away...
dissipate into thin air like I was never even here.

If I could catch em', I'd bottle them up,
I'm afraid to say I'd needed more than a cup,
to hold the years of agony I've faced,
The ugly past I wish to erase.

Each one that falls has a story of its own,
keeping the earth moist,
If caught I know they'd voice,
my anger, my pride, my hurt deep inside,
oh how I've cried,
my pain, my shame, my good name I'd defamed.

Day after day, year after year,
a river was formed on account of a tear-
that fell from my eyes and rolled to my thigh
I covered my face, hanging my head in disgrace.

71

Quite a debacle I had made
and now I must face
tasting the salt from each tear,
each one I could hear . . . screaming.

Haunted by each crime
I trace back in time on their memory line,
only to find each drop was Divine
appointed for such a time as this.

I tell you if tears could talk, they'd speak well of me,
saying daughter, we used you that you might see.

Real life was unfolding right before my face. Not only did I now have two babies with two different men, but I was still not married, and thus had to prove paternity by taking a DNA test. I was mortified. This left me in panic mode. I was scared because I still had not found my own life, yet was responsible for two others. Although I had now had the experience of giving birth twice, I still had not gone down the aisle in my white dress, or experienced the true love of a husband. There was no honeymoon. I felt as though I owed back all of those years and poor decisions I made in my youth that caused so much turmoil. I knew in a lifetime I couldn't fix it, so I would just become a doormat until I felt like I'd collected as much dirt back that I had dealt out. I felt dirty, unworthy, and undeserving.

I had not until that point ever walked in who I was. I didn't even know who I was even though others' seemed to. I believe it was intimidating at times. I believe I was in the fight of my life. I was kept to think I "was not" when really, "I *was*!" I thought I couldn't stand alone, think alone, be alone, create alone, provide alone, or excel alone. What I didn't come to find out until now was that I was never alone! I had the love, spirit, heart and mind of Jesus in my soul. Everything that I am and was to be, I was already. Equipped before birth with greatness! Jeremiah 1:5

At this point, I had to ask myself. What will I do with what I'd gone through and learned? How will I make it effective in the Kingdom of God? This is the more that we should be striving for. We have the ability to take our hardships and make the road that much easier or at least clearer for the next individual. The goal is to fight and help prepare the generations to come. It's called *legacy*!

Through these experiences, we are able to learn much about ourselves. We are able to learn our strengths from our weaknesses. We find out our fears and mature in our gifts. We are able to see ourselves for more than where we've been but, in turn, begin to equip ourselves for where we are going. We learn not to lock ourselves into categorical boxes, nor limit the dimensions of our walls nor depths of our ceilings. We are open to the creator as vessels to use as He sees fit. No one can define you. We are not words in a dictionary collected, lined up and placed in alphabetical order to be read, defined and understood. It is our mission to simply trust in the Lord. We, instead, are more like clay and pliable to the need of the Master's hand. Only He knows the beginning and the end. We are a continual work in progress and not limited to the likes of man but that of our Father's plan.

~

Once presented with the statement, "I didn't know that you were a writer," I replied, "I am many things. A daughter, a granddaughter, a mother, a mentor, an educator, a friend, a vocalist, an actress, a model, a minister of the Word of God, a former police officer, a NCAA Division #1 basketball player and coach, a behavioral therapist, and so on. But most of all, I am a child of God!" In God, I am not limited to who I am or can become. Neither are you. I am a messenger of the Word of God, in whatever way I can get that message through. There are many ways in which His people can and will be reached. I have tried other ways and won't stop trying until I have exhausted all means. Writing is one way in which I will attempt to reach the world one page, one story, one whisper, one word, one heartbeat, one laugh, and one tear at a time. So, Yes, I am a writer.

On top of all else, God has given me to partake in, I have decided to write.... well share what I have written. I have actually always written. You know, a paper here, a paper there, be it scribbling lines on tissue, the back of long receipts or even on offering envelopes found in my Bible, Oops! Many days, that was the only offering I had. I have just never pieced anything together. It is kind of like my life, fragmented, in pieces and everywhere. It was now time to pull it all in, pull it all together, make some sense of all of this non-sense and see if I couldn't find an ounce or more of meaning to it. Writing, for me, has also proven to be a healthy attempt to download a compilation of a lifetime of experiences, all floating around, vying for position in my life as to ascertain and/or define who I am...a constant battle in itself, for none will ever gain the right to totally define me, as this life we live is just that; a life. Life is a journey that will take a lifetime to travel.

We will constantly grow in our spiritual genetics, change shape and form several times before the face of man, proving that God is alive and real, before we return to the earth from whence we came. We were born to bloom!

I am learning in my later years to release into the atmosphere what may help or bless someone else. It is not necessarily for my benefit or demise but that which the higher calling has directed me to do. Because ownership belongs to God and not me, I am free to release with lack of fear and judgment. Now, that is a freeing experience. To be free at 40 is something I welcome with open arms.

Writing has been a vehicle, one of several in my life, in which I am able to corporately express myself for the greater good of not just Jaz, but mankind itself, if received. I am careful, however, not to label or limit myself to any one particular domain. In this way, God can use me in any way He sees fit. I write, not as a way to escape reality, as I used to but, rather, to grasp and embrace God *as my reality* as I pen for His glory!

I have spent a lifetime in search of who I am, instead of who He is and who I am in Him. This is a chapter inspired by the beauty that surrounds us on a daily basis, not only the beauty that lies deep within our souls but that which we overlook in a world of hustle and bustle. We, oftentimes, are so quick to get somewhere we were never meant to be, only to realize that what we are trying to become, we already are.

For we are His workmanship, created in Christ Jesus for good works, which God prepared beforehand that we should walk in them.(Ephesians 2:10)

CHAPTER SEVEN

Born to Bloom

We were born to bloom, you see, seeded from the very beginning to become what we will eventually be. It is a process, but we'll get there if we keep living and allow God to feed, water and shine on us. There was a point where I couldn't see my way through the vines, the dirt, the muck and mire. Not so! I've been planted in the earth to bloom as a flower. I was born to bloom! Germination is yet a season. I had been rooted and grounded in the Word but had not realized nor connected with the switch that activated the light. The Son!

According to Colossians 3:10, I have put on a new man. I am renewed in knowledge according to the image of Him who created Him. And it is my responsibility to let my light shine so that others will come to know Christ as their personal Lord and Savior.

Let your light so shine before men that they may see your good works and glorify the father which lives in heaven. (Matthew 5:16)

I am a flower! I was born to bloom, not to stay in the dirt forever covered by darkness and despair smothered in manure. When I realized the God-given ability that was within me to leave a tangible mark on the world for good, I began to utilize my ability to shift gears. A car runs and will run you into a wall, off the road or even over a bridge but for the fact that you have control of the steering wheel. How many of us already know this? Thus the saying, *Let God take the wheel.* The power to shift our thinking is a crucial point of reference. The ability to take control over our direction in life, to choose to be led by the Holy Spirit and not to have to wonder through the wilderness, is a beautiful thing to have. Now that's something to shout about! Praise break!

We have to learn to see it before we see it, as my Minister of Music, Elder Ron Rosson, used to say and sing. I had to begin to see, have vision, that is, learn to see the light even in the dark, envisioning the outcome before the beginning. I am reminded of boys of all ages growing up. When I coached in the

NCAA women's basketball league, I used to tell my players to watch the boys. I asked them how many had little brothers, cousins or nephews? Do you remember when they'd be out in the backyard talking to themselves? They'd pretend they were in an arena packed with thousands of people all cheering for them, *only them*! They'd look their imaginary opponents in the eye with the look of hungry lions, who only had one end in mind...*victory*! Then they'd begin the countdown...as they professed out aloud every move they would make along the way adding in their own name.

It went something like this:

"Here comes Strange! Down the court she dribbles the ball. She crosses her defender over, makes a power move, spins left and elevates into the air high over her opponent, the fans go crazy screaming!!! HAAAAAAAAA! 5...4...3...2...1.... She releases the ball and *"Scores!"* Confetti everywhere, the stands go wild!"

Who doesn't remember this? It's called *having vision*...when you can see the end from the beginning and are able to not only see but talk your way through it.

Those able to master the art of vision could hold up under pressure in the real game because they had been there many times before and could see themselves from a victorious position (even if only in their minds). Well, the same goes for us, the children of God, who have the mindset of Christ. We are to see ourselves as victorious as the angels cheer for us from heaven, showering down, not confetti but blessings, as we live out the intended plan and purpose for our lives. I myself had to learn to see (have vision) in the spirit that I had not yet seen in the physical in order for it to manifest itself in the *now* which already was and is.

Now faith is the substance of things hoped for, the evidence of things not seen. (Hebrews 11:1)

The seed, as you've already heard it so many times before, be it in church or elsewhere, has already been planted. According to the life of a flower, there is a process that must take place before reaching its proposed outcome; thus, my study of the flower in its parallel to the growth in our lives here on earth.

And so *the light came on!* This was me! Jasmine, a flower in the process of blooming... Not only was my name a flower, I thought to myself, but my life resembled one as well. Delicate, precious, sweet, fragrant, yet bitter if you bite it, strong rooted and though my petals shift direction and wither frequently, they always grow back even the more beautiful. To me, this was a simple reminder that something that beautiful was never meant to be bit. A flower exudes the essence of peace and is totally dependent upon God for its very existence. Though flowers are passed daily many times, yet not acknowledged, they are very beautiful to the ones that take a minute to stop and witness one of God's loveliest creations.

> *I am a rose of Sharon, a lily of the valley.*
> (Song of Solomon 2:11)

I had lost much, desperately scrambling to gain it back, and, at the very least, not lose it all again. I finally took time to stop and smell the roses, taking time to view and witness one of God's many creations. Literally, I stopped and smelled them as my car, at this point, had broken down for the umpteenth time and walking became a way of life for my children and I. I saw things I had never before seen or maybe I had seen and I had never paid attention to. Walking daily now in the 100 degree plus weather caused me to do this instead. Now that the truck had completely died, just as the lilies I hadn't considered, I was blessed to come upon a lesson or two on God and the Bible, which I always enjoyed. It would be a day that I walked my son home from summer camp, down Ventura Avenue, as I was now doing quite frequently. My son, sweat dripping from his nose, was dragging his feet and completely dehydrated. I assured him we'd be home soon, at least another two blocks or so. He pleaded that we stop! I am sure my daughter, now 17, can relate as she too (over a decade ago) may as well remember a season of walking with mommy.

"Hey, isn't that Mr. Guy's house?", my son asked. "Can we please ask him for something to drink?"

"No, boy." I said with a frustrating tone. "We have drinks at home."

Cadence looked so sad as we continued to trudge our way home, until we heard a familiar voice. "Hey, you all want to sit down and get something to drink?" It was almost as if he could read my poor boy's face and his momma's heart. I smiled timidly, saying, "well, we're almost home, but my boy could use a drink."

Talk about full circle. I could count on Old' Man Charles to be in his garage every day seated in his lazy boy watching life pass by thinking back over his own, while warning us young people of life's red flags and the consequences that would surely follow. He, too, was walking, breathing wisdom. It was a double-edged sword. I believe that he lived for this stage in his life, being 80 years plus, with much to share.

Isn't that just how life is. We so need one another, whether we admit to it or not. We were tired in more ways than one, thirsty and on empty. I could tell by his demeanor that he, too, was exhausted and possibly, in a different sense, thirsty and empty as well. We served each other on that day well.

I shared with him how I had been trying to force myself into spaces I just did not fit. I tried to make myself something by way of a name, title, man, job or otherwise. I was hurt each time and rejected by lack of space for my presence. I felt weak, alone, out of control, angry, sad, depressed and incapable. I had second-guessed everything I was or could be. Despair and distain was beginning to take over. I began to give my life slowly over to the world, my wounded heart, my soul, my body, my money, my time, my energy, my very existence was dissipating before my very eyes. Things began to fold and completely shut down. My man, my job, garbage, water, food, my truck, of course, my relationship with God dimming, hope fading, and the lights went out!

Feeling my way through the dark, I had nothing but time on my hands since I had no job. Degreed and all, all of those past silver plate experiences, nothing could help save me now -- good looks, charm, smarts, a pretty voice that had once gotten me by...*nothing*! Everywhere I went I was forced to walk, having no car and all. It forced me to slow down and take in all of what made up the most basic, the most natural, the most beautiful of creations all dependent on God.. Praise be unto God. I do know Him! I know enough that He instilled something somewhere, somehow, someway, someday that I could grab "holt" to, as my grandma used to say. I just didn't know when nor how to go about getting it. As long as I'd been in church, as long as I'd been leading praise and worship, and telling others how good God was and what all He could do, I didn't know how to get it from Him for myself.

I pointed people to the can and even the can opener, the key to access the food, but had no idea how that thing really worked. When it came time for me to use it, I didn't know how. I was stuck, left hungry and thirsty. I had bottles upon bottles of food I could not open. I so desperately needed them to survive. Even though I had had it all along, the can, the food and the opener, I did not have the knowledge, courage or strength to access it on my own. Supply, Supplier and Me; a book in itself.

So I walked and I walked and every step I took, I kid you not, I saw a rose. Though my phone lacked service, it would still take pictures. I have the times and dates to prove it. I began to document everything from that point forward. It was a sign to me. It was like a lifeline. These roses were in all different colors. Call me crazy, but get this, I didn't realize roses came in all those different colors. I began to ask God, why? Why am I running into all of these flowers? "You're not running into them," He replied, "They have been there all along." Oops, I said, "Well why am I observing all of them now?" He answered and I still have chills all over my body. "Because you have finally taken the time out to seek My face. I am them and they are Me. You now have the keys to appreciate life. Because you see Me, you see *life*! Because of Me, they have life. Because of Me, so do you."

Jesus said to him, "I am the way, the truth, and the life. No one comes to the Father except through Me. (John 14:6)

"Not only do you have life, but with Me and in Me, you will have it more abundantly!"

"Oh, My! You mean that song I've been singing to so many people for so long? "Yes" by Shekinah Glory. Yes! I do see you! Not only do I see you, but I can hear you! I can feel you! Tell me more God! Walk with me! Talk to me!"

I had found an immediate place of comfort. Nothing yet had changed necessarily on the outside, but my inside was at total peace. I knew I would be alright. I knew I was with God and He with me. I began taking pictures every day for the remainder of that summer until my phone began to fill up. I now have a collection of hundreds of pictures of bloomed flowers from that summer, a reminder of my encounter with God.

The beautiful flowers in my neighborhood from my cell phone collection, like me, like us, they exist, have life, depend on God for their every need to be met on that day. Everything that they need to sustain life comes from God. They are all so very unique and individually and magnificently made. Just like you and me.

Consider the lilies, how they grow: they neither toil nor spin; and yet I say to you, even Solomon in all his glory was not arrayed like one of these. (Luke 12:27)

I was visited by the Holy Spirit, which spoke this to me. "Consider me, and I will take care of you, just as I've taken care of them. You are beautiful beyond your own recognition. Now that you have recognized the beauty in them, you must now recognize it within your own being. That is where it all starts; within you! Stop looking outside of you to find you. Everything you will ever need to sustain a productive long lasting beautiful and fruitful life was seeded at conception to be birthed in its season to ripen and/or bloom according to its own unique design and in its own unique and perfect time."

"Being confident of this very thing, that He who has begun a good work in you will complete it until the day of Jesus Christ."
Philippians 1:6

"Doth thou know who you are? Doth thou know from whence you come? Doth thou realize whose you are? He is that He is!" If He is, then we are! No longer surrounded by dirt, dark, and manure, but a physical manifestation of God's glorious beauty. Everywhere I look, I see Him now. I hear Him now. I feel Him. I feel Him because I carry Him. He in me and I in Him. Surely as I am writing today, butterflies surround me and shuffle through the flowers like a mini air force air show, back and forth they dart, doing fancy tricks. They flutter their wings, displaying their beautiful colors and simply enjoying life. A fly just landed on my hand. I sit still until it buzzes off as a respect to my Lord. In that, I reverence all that He has made and take the time on this day to take it all in, allowing life to take its course without being rushed or shooed away. The ducks are gliding on the lake water, the turtles sit upon a rock baking in the sun. The fat coy fish lie just beneath the surface of the water. Up above, the birds chirp and sing in competition with the laughter of the children playing in the near distance. A Mariachi Band sets up to one side of me as I sit barefoot amongst the grass, and an old man sits on a bench with his dog on the other side. We are all here! As we operate in our own vein, we share the wind, the sun and misty sprays across the waterfall that spurts up and plunges back into the lake.

A lady just came out . . .

"It looks like you're in Paris or somewhere. You have an aura around you that I can't explain," she said, "I had to come over and get some of it," speaking of the beautiful surroundings we were experiencing. I replied, "I know. I was just sitting here writing about it. No one is going to believe me, but you have just confirmed it," smiling at her with pure joy as she began walking away.

"Have a nice day," she called out.

"Oh I am and I will." Thank you, I replied as she went on her way.

Apparently my awakening had not only begun on the inside, but was now recognized from the out. What a beautiful revelation this was. I was headed on the right track.

CHAPTER EIGHT

Pleased . . . as Peaches!

It would be New Year's Eve that I'd receive a text that would propel me into my next wave of life, taking me into yet another downward spiral. I was doing well, so I thought, beginning to heal and recover from the most recent of my life endeavors. I'd turned my life completely over to the Lord. By this time, I was not only in the choir, but leading praise and worship at my church, directing the youth choir and even the adult choir on a paid status as well as teaching Sunday school. What an honor to be bestowed upon me. I felt as though my obedience was opening doors for me. I wore my skirts to the floor and allowed no man to the door!

Klink, Klink, as Tyler Perry would say. Madea would often teach the young ladies this technique shutting down any invitation of the opposite sex. I was on a roll! I had my horse blinders on and everything. My initial focus was on the hills from whence cometh my help because up until then, I had clearly been weak, possessing not one strong bone in me. I set myself up so tough that it felt as if people were waiting for me to fall. All eyes were on me because no one could be that perfect. A friend of mine used to always ask could he pinch me to see if I was real. I tried my hardest to prove them wrong! I was happy but for a moment in time. I felt at peace, I felt an inner joy. I had my daughter now in grade school and my son in pre-school. Starting to heal and now standing straight again, especially after the birth of my son by a man so young and in a town so small, I was standing steadfast. If a man was going to be a part of us, he was going to have to join this family totally!

I attended a night service one New Year's Eve. It was good, really good. The spirit of the Lord was in me. Don't you know that is when you are tried the most? Before I begin this next journey, be it clear that people are not the enemy for we don't fight flesh. It is the spirit that lingers searching for a body to dwell that we must pay closest attention to, pray for and war against if necessary. In no way are any of my experiences with people that of me coming across an enemy. I loved and still love everyone referenced in this book and can only pray they love me too. God is love. However, the spirit of the enemy came in between each of our dealings and I personally was not strong enough for the both of us in any of the situations to fight him off, leaving both myself and the other party open and subject to abuse and ultimate failure over and over again. We all have freedom in our own decision-making and this is why having a clear, confident surefooted clean and healthy state of mind is important. This will ensure that our walk with the Lord be whole, holy and righteous, so that we can walk with our heads held high as we carry on to victory. The goal is to be fruitful and multiply, not to tear down, deceive and divide.

And God blessed them, saying, "Be fruitful and multiply, and fill the waters in the seas, and let birds multiply on the earth. (Genesis 1:22)

Carrying on, as I praised, prayed and worshipped, I felt a tingling on my body, no really, it was on my lap. It was my cell phone vibrating. It was a text. Knowing, in church, I shouldn't be looking at my phone…I still did. It read, "Is this Jasmine?" To that, I responded, "Yes." It was a young man I'd met some months ago prior. A drop dead gorgeous man at that! He was a man that made my heart flutter, my insides beam, my body quiver, and my eyes glean. Yeah….one of those. I blushed like I was a child again, feelin' somethin' I wasn't supposed to be feelin.' I could not look him directly in the face, I took deep breathes when he was near, and my ears perked like that of a dog at the very sound of his name...yeah....one of those. They don't come around often, but when they do ... Well, let's just say he had my full and undivided attention. But what could he possibly want from me?

The last I had spoken to him he was trying to maintain a relationship with the mother of his youngest two children. How beautiful was that? Mind you, I was at this point in life, although on my way back up, feeling like damaged goods, you see, so I had no room for judgment of another at this time. Well, even though at the time I first met him, I couldn't have him, that gained him so much respect in my book and, seeing as though he already had favor in my eyes, gave him brownie points galore. You see, he made it clear that he was interested but responsibly had to do what was best for his family unit at that time. I agreed wholeheartedly. Time lapsed and on this day, the 2ndof January I'd hear from him again.

Who might this be, I asked? He replied with his name. My heart sunk into my shoes...mind you, I courted this guy a bit prior to rekindling, but he never made it past my front porch. I would always come out, sit with him and talk. Often, he'd ride up on his motorcycle and park. Again, we'd giggle and gleam at each other. We'd be on the phone till' the wee hours of the morning till I'd fall asleep with phone in hand. I'd even seen my picture on his phone as a screen saver once, one of the highest honors for a young lady in my not yet fully healed state of mind lol, It was so special, one of those memories I wished I could bottle forever. Though in heart it will always be with me.

His text would follow with the request to see me. I truly believe from the respect he had given me from the above mentioned encounters, he gained a direct pass in without passing *go*! In the midst of the text conversation, I never stopped once to think why he was reaching out now and/or what may have become of the relationship with the mother of his children. I guess that happens when you want something as bad as I did, and *he*.... I *wanted*!

Date night, was a movie night. We watched "Boys to Men". This was a date in fact that did not end until some three years later. Roller coaster of a lifetime, but it was my roller coaster with my name on it and at the time, I was so happy to be on it, rush after rush. The highest of the highs and the lowest of the lows that I think I had ever experienced. The interesting part to me was the fact that we had no children together and even in our sin, no mishaps either, *truly it was a soul tie*. One in which would prove to be the most consuming one of my life. And so the saga begins...

He came for the movie and swaddled me tight. I knew I had found my life soul mate. He was a keeper. Together, like Bonnie and Clyde, we would fight off the world. In my eyes, he could do *no* wrong, and I, proudly became his ride or die chick.

Extreme opposites, he would teach me the streets do's and don'ts and protect me, like I always wanted to be. And I..., I would supposedly lead him to a better way of life. Together we would beat all the odds. Or so we thought. Needless to say, I didn't take into consideration once again anything of his past nor did I consider that of mine that I was still supposedly healing from. Nevertheless, it is *he* that would ultimately aid in my healing process, though not in the way I expected.

I'd again self-medicate with that good old' medicine I'd been introduced to at 13. Wow! I have chills, writing and recovering all at the same time looking outside in and viewing my journey from a different perspective. He made me happy. He made me feel safe. He made me feel needed. I was needed more by this man than any one in my life. Over time, all else would fail, but I would remain needed by him to this day.

As I was saying, his first night over would be the day/night he'd move into my home and enter my soul forever. I didn't see it coming, didn't realize it happening, nor did I fight it. All I cared about was that *he* was there. He'd show up the next day and again the next day. I was "pleased as peaches" as my grandma would say. What does that mean anyway? The very fact that he would come back after "you know what", to me meant the world. I was not used to them returning the day after for fear of the dreaded commitment that is expected after an act of that nature. The men I was with would usually be what we call ghost in the wind. We would be friends at best.

What I thought was genuine love finally being shown toward me, was actually exile from the ex and baby mama. Though I had his things, she had his heart. Physically, he was there daily. Mentally, he was not. He'd become bitter as the days would pass on. I could sense he was feeling trapped because he'd met me, a beautiful and sweet, Christian girl who took him in completely. I was totally unaware that he did not truly love me and sensed he was obligated to live up to a pedestal that could never be reached. Due to the immediate exile from his last place of residence, he came with a boat load of baggage.

This was not only physical boxes and bins, but mental and emotional pains and experiences, too. There was a plethora of agony that he had suppressed. Sound familiar? Yeah, he was a splitting image of me! We were mirrors and magnets of and to one another both attracted and propelled on any given day, dependent upon the direction our magnets were facing. This would prove to be our soul tie. That is, with no real home base, struggling to find not only ourselves, but a place to call home inside of another instead of inside of the Lord, continually hurting all that would come into contact with us. We were co-dependent to the thousandth power! I needed to love and he needed someone to love him. It didn't matter where I went, he'd find me, or where he'd stray, when he returned, I'd let him in.

This was a vicious cycle that had taken the circuitous route for far too many times.

Now where was I? Day by day, his things would move in. What I hadn't mentioned was that at the time, I had already begun my move out. I had a plan prior to rekindling with this man. Most of all of my things were in storage. As my things continued to move outward, his were coming in. My plan was to take the income tax money I had coming and to move myself and the kids into a bigger home and better place to live. Well, when my partner in crime entered into my life, I became paralyzed by his presence and his need, which ultimately fed my need. My original goal shifted from my plan, my needs, my children's needs, to his. He knows this and in all fairness to him, he's always asked that I not do that, but . . .

I would then spend my entire tax check just to keep us afloat, all 4 of us. Somebody reading this knows what I'm talking about and I'm sure others are like "YOU DID WHAAAAAAT??? Here is where I need an Emoji face or three. It was just so comforting having someone there that I lost track of all I was doing and thinking. I was simply living in the moment and thinking in the moment. I was gone during the days working my lil' touchy off as I'd done my entire life. He'd stay home helping with things around the house, my mess, and filling out applications for school and possible jobs. Did I say mess? One of the many reasons I later lost him "MY MESS"!.

Remember, I said in the beginning of this book I would need a housekeeper. I wasn't lying! The day came when during one of his cleaning sprees', he found my glock40/21calliber firearm from when I was a police officer. This began yet another stream of legal issues that would soon entangle not only he, but myself as well.

I attended work as I had done every other day. After clocking out, I was immediately surrounded by several police cars before I could get out of my job's parking lot. They circled my car and treated me like the worst criminal ever, looking in through the windows with cupped hands as if to find a body or something. Slowly they crept around my truck. I had never been so humiliated. I, scared to death, didn't know what was going on. They, the officers, told me I had paper in my windshield and it could slide, obstruct my view and be dangerous while driving. Ok, I was a prior cop. That had nothing to do with the stop and search, but ok, I wasn't arguing. I just assumed my boyfriend had to use my truck and had used it enough to be recognized and linked to him. Eventually, the police let me go saying, "Have a nice day!" I was still puzzled.

When I returned home, hours would pass and no sign of my boyfriend. I'd receive several calls that I paid no mind to from the correctional facility asking me if I would take a collect call. I just assumed they had the wrong number, until I heard his voice on the phone stating his name. Oh my word! *What is going on?* I thought. My man! The only piece of love I thought I had, aside from my children and family which is an altogether different love, was gone! He was now in jail, locked up behind bars. This could not be. He had been picked up for possessing the gun he had found in my home. So, of course, I felt a sense of responsibility for that, though I shouldn't. I never got it back, the firearm that is, and didn't fight it either, out of shame for lack of responsibility in the entire ordeal. I was operating with an unhealed mindset. The ploy was, "you need to get me out of here."

"You want your man home, don't you?" *My heart melted.*

"Yes, I do."

"Then I need you to bail me out!"

Huh? Bail? This was foreign territory to me. I had *never* dealt with anything like this before.

In this timeframe, I would meet G-Pa. Face to face that is... G-Pa was my boyfriend's father. Up until this point, I had only spoken with him briefly on the phone when he tried numerous times to reach out to his son. He wanted only the best for his boy and would call daily like clockwork looking for him, checking on him to make sure he was ok, had money, food to eat and courage in his heart. His daddy spoke life into him and instilled a sense of hope. He would daily offer him jobs or request that they put their heads together to form a family business. You see, his dad was an entrepreneur. He had always been in business for himself, be it professional ball or the local town pool hall he opened and ran. G-Pa had a side business painting addresses on the curbs of people's homes and he asked daily for him to run it. He tried desperately to give him a sense of manhood that the world would not altogether consume his boy. My boyfriend, although appreciative, desired and was determined to make it on his own. Sounds funny to hear myself call him that, "boyfriend", because I had an inkling that I was just one of his 4 or 5 houses that he had privy to. I'll address that later.

Now back in jail, yes, back in jail! You see, I never background checked my beautiful eyed curly headed man. Apparently, this, for him, was nothing new. Needing a way out, he called me. He requested first that I seek out his father who, at the time, was in the hospital. He gave me his direct line and said go to the hospital and get money to bail me out. I went. I met G-Pa in person for the very first time after several phone call conversations we'd had. He welcomed me into the room questioning immediately my status with his son. I proudly said that I was his girlfriend. He asked was I sure? Along with many other questions, as if he did not quite believe the validity of any of my answers.

I, without any inside information, had to carry on and feel my way through the dialogue. G-Pa eventually warmed up to me. I believe this was due to feeling my heart, genuine spirit and love for his son, He said, "sit down." So, I did just that and took a seat at the foot of his bed. "Listen, he said, I love my son more than anything in this world, but I am tired. I just can't do this anymore; I've bailed him out before." Huh? What had I gotten into? Tears began to fall from my eyes. I wanted my "boyfriend" home and safe. I kindly thanked G-Pa and left realizing this man was now attached to me and I to him, a bond we would share until the end.

My boyfriend would then direct me to the local bondsmen in town. My introduction to the world of "Lock Up" had been presented. I felt with the lack of traditional motherly upbringing, leaving him to be raised by his grandmother, then passed on, and a father who later became terminally ill, he had no one. I made a commitment from that point forward to be with him always. I was determined to be his back bone, his rock, his ride or die chick for lack of better phrasing, to be his . . . just *his* period.

I took my income tax money and placed it down for his bail, paying the remainder off little by little from each paycheck. Signing the paper work seemed more in depth than buying a car, house or even life insurance. It would forever attach my name to something that I, myself, would never imagine being involved in. It linked my name to a life I knew nothing about. I had only seen, "Dog the Bounty Hunter" up until that point and was scared to death that at any time someone would be coming to get me if I didn't pay his bail or was late on my payments. Mind you, I had still not moved into my own place, a place that I would not be seeing anytime soon. The money had been spent.

I recall a day I showed to court and painfully watched as they escorted my boyfriend in. He was handcuffed and in a yellow full body jumpsuit. He could barely look me in the face. I'm sure not wanting me to ever see him like this. I was clearly upset, get this, not at him but at the judge for doing what actually was his job. My sense of thinking was tremendously warped. I scowled at the judge and cop, angry that they had taken a part of what I thought made me whole. Bail would be set and I would cover it. I arrived at the jail for the first time, I had no idea this would soon become a common place to me. I hopped out of the car feeling like somebody. It was this artificial sense of belonging to something, to someone, to a cause that was bigger than me, well at least over my head.

I pulled with me a large chain belonging to his dog, who ended up in my care in the meanwhile. Penny, a Pitt Bull. I felt so cool. I was in this world that I had never been in before, nor did I belong, but played the role as best I could. The closest I had ever come to this experience was when I tried out for the role of the "gangsta" girlfriend in the movie, "The Principal" when I was in high school. I actually got a call back for the role but had no parental consent, as I tried out without the knowledge of my mother. "Smh," as the kids today would say. Nevertheless, I approached the entrance. I was stopped by the sheriff, asking if he could help me. I informed him that I was there to pick up my boyfriend. He looked puzzled and asked who? I gave him his first and last name, then watched his face drop. Mine did too, but in puzzlement. The sheriff let me know that he wasn't quite ready and proceeded to talk to me until he came out. He asked, "Ma'am, do you mind if I ask how'd you get with him? I mean, I don't mean any disrespect, but looking at you and talking to you, you don't appear to be, well... I just don't get how... I cocked my head sideways waiting for what he had to say about my man. He finished with...well.. just how you two got together. That's all". That's all? He just totally offended me and my guy. He continued by saying, " I know him well and . . ." Out he came! I ran into his arms feeling closer to him than ever. I didn't care two hill of beans about anything that I would later come to realize as being unequally yoked. I *loved* him.

I don't know if it was the contract binding bail, meeting dad, the fact that he now lived with me, or the need to be needed that pulled me even the closer to him. I felt as if we were almost contracted, kind of like you are in a marriage with documents that tie you together. I decided to go all the way in. I gave myself completely over to him. Mind, body and soul.

Driving home, we locked eyes.

"What?" he said.

"I feel like I'm going to be with you forever," I answered with a gleam of light in my eyes.

He said, "I do too. You will teach me . . . and I will teach you," with a tone I'll always remember. Again, I melted.

They say when a man speaks, listen to him. The street is exactly what I learned. I was so head over heels for this guy, I couldn't hear, think or see straight. We were both damaged and needing a place to belong, a heart to call home. I gave him my heart, but it found no home. Daily, I am getting it back.

Once back home, I helped to see that he got into school. He applied and got in. We did what we had to do to make it work. I didn't mind investing because this was the man I would be with for always. I considered it all in the family. If he was built up, he would be even the stronger to hold us up, for this now was the man of our family, so I thought. He even helped my kids with homework assignments, projects, fixed their toys and somehow retrieved a bike someone had stolen in the neighborhood that belonged to my daughter. Oh yeah, I was *in* love! His school was an hour or so away and on public transportation maybe even two. It was costly with the commute alone back and forth, but it was worth it. Between he, G-Pa and myself, we made it happen.

Things can hold you captive if you allow them to, as I once was, until I broke free from that in which was unhealthy for me and compromised my walk with Christ. There came a time when staying nearer to the school became more beneficial in his eyes. He had a cousin there he could stay with. We were getting closer and closer you see and I don't believe that is what he wanted. Mind you, he still had three children with moms with unresolved relations.

Now, being financially connected to me, I believe he felt a sense of obligation. What I mistook for love was actually guilt and obligation. I held on as long as I could because I felt he needed a place to come home to, a place to call home; never mind the fact my kids and I would find ourselves homeless in a couple of weeks.

I'm a Good Girl!

CHAPTER NINE

I'm a Good Girl!

Have you ever noticed the power that comes in situations when we are barren? Times when our backs are against the wall and there's no direction we can seem to turn for help. If you are still reading this book, you are here. This is because He is here with us. The good Lord, that is. When we can no longer stand, He carries us. When we can no longer see, He gives us vision. When we can no longer breath, He blows the wind of life back into us. He is God and God alone. Alone, we do great damage. However, in Him we cannot fail! Joel 3:10 says, "Let the weak say I am strong." I have been the most powerful when I had nothing and relied on God, who had everything, and been the weakest when I thought I had it all, but lacked God. There were times I was working a full time job, making good money, and still could not seem to make ends meet. Seems I'd made enough to cover it all, but somehow at the end of the month, it just didn't add up! Further and further, I began digging myself into debt. Again, this was with steady income coming in bi-weekly.

It is in the absence of the physical and worldly things we rely on *that we find our true self*, need, worth, ability, purpose and calling. It is when the world quiets down and you are unable to pull on the outward source of anything or anyone that you have to dig down deep within to pull. When you realize your source for living is actually found inside. God, the gift that lives in you, your Healer, your Redeemer, your Comforter, your Provider, your Way Maker, your Guide and ultimate life support. It is not until you are weak that you desire to become strong. When the water runs out, you thirst. When vision departs, you dream. When the boat sinks, you will reach upward. Thank God for His lifeline of rescue! He is waiting for you!

As long as you reside in comfort, you will never move into who you truly are.

There was a time when the dollar bill did not come as easily as it once did. Silver spoon turned into wood overnight. Due to situations I caused of carelessness, poor planning, mismanagement of money, poor decision-making and a simple lack of funds, I'd landed myself and my children in the unthinkable, a women and children's shelter. I shared earlier, several things, decisions and circumstances that led to this point. It is not the things that landed us here that I am focusing on, but the *amazing* way God took care of us through that season. He did us like He does the flowers and the birds by providing our daily bread. I have no better way to thank *Him, The Almighty Master* than to share of His goodness and kindness toward us.

It is a sad moment to see and experience the look of your children's faces when you are unable to properly provide for them. They have no one else to look to but you for proper guidance and caretaking, knowing and expecting that you will get the job done right. You sigh…then make up stories, rock them, sing them to sleep, then pray. I can recall staying up all night in my truck as we lived in prior to getting into the shelter. I refused to fall asleep as to make sure my son would be safe and free from any apparent danger as he'd slumber until morning came. I remained awake nodding off every now and again until the stars passed and the sun appeared. Anguish in my heart, I'd drive to the McDonald's where we'd wash up prior to dropping my son off to summer camp and carrying myself on to work.

Yes, it was surreal. No one would believe it, just like the Pursuit of Happiness movie, no lie. I thank my co-worker and friend, Nisa, for providing and bringing undergarments to me prior to my shift. You never realize the humbling things you may have to experience in this life.

That same desperation was there as I had to keep a steady look of confidence and comfort upon my face not having a clue as to my next steps. Fortunately, my eldest daughter was in Chicago for this portion of hell…but she'd soon return to experience some of the same woes…

My son, who thought this was the most exciting venture ever, completely countered the response of my teen daughter, who had tears streaming from her eyes down her cheeks. The neighbors we encountered in the facility, who were like shelter hoppers, quickly schooled my daughter in the blessings that she had. It was a bit harsh, I have to say, as they were in her face similar to that you'd see on the reality show *"Scared Straight"*. They informed her how spoiled they thought she was, as she rolled in the facility stepping out of a Ford truck with her permed hair, skinny jeans, new shoes and the like, not wanting to touch anything or anyone to touch her. She looked at me, as to say, "How could you have failed us like this?" For the first time, I, the woman of so many words, had very little to say. I was in so much pain and I was ashamed. I couldn't speak. This was unimaginable. She had school projects that needed group sessions to complete, you know when the kids get together at one another's homes, however, no one could come where we were, and it was so very hard to get out because you needed permission slips in advance to be filled out, approved and signed in advance.

I remember the day I told the shelter manager I was going to InShape (a local gym), as I always did in my daily routine. They said, "No you're not. We eat dinner at 6:00 p.m. We have chapel at 7:00 p.m. and AA at 8:00 p.m." "Excuse me? I'm not eating here," I thought to myself, and I already go to church. Oh, and I'm definitely not going to anybody's AA meeting! Thank God I didn't have any addictions (so I thought).

But that wasn't the case for many of the women who were living there. Clearly, I was in denial, *big* time for it was my addiction to men, dysfunctional relations and mismanagement of money that landed me there. That's when I realized my problem was just as *big* as any of the ladies there. It didn't have to be drugs, alcohol or prostitution. There are many ways in which one could prostitute themselves and I had mastered one. I just dressed it up in a face of pretend.

The Face of Pretend

What lies behind the painted faces we wear?
The clothes we pick out,
The selected things we share,
The tormented spirits that guide us there

Behind the scenes there lies a dare,
To go? To stay? To know? To obey?
Life or death…
Which do you choose on this day?
I choose life ~ so I kneel before thee,
To pray for a covering ~ a shield ~
To keep the enemy away,
For there's so much more I've got to say . . .

Just know I can't go out this way…

No! Not today!
Not this way!
So I stand to fight with all of my might!
I remove the pillow from my head

That smothers light~
From entering my soul
While disrupting my plight…
Can't take no more of this tight-----

Choke on my neck from the devils' bite!
Release me! I say!
I just got to' get away,
From this clench of the wicked

Who hunts me like prey,
But there comes a day,
Oh, yeah, that's judgment day,
Where the people must stand

Stand up and say,
This is not me, this fake,
False grin, it just hides all the pain,
That's locked up inside

My mask comes off,
I reveal my soul,
The time has come,
My story be tol'

Rewind

When I was younger, all I wanted to be was a mom, a wife and to have a family unit. That was exactly what I wanted. My father informed me that it didn't matter what I wanted to become, even if it was to become a *prostitute*, as long as I was the best at it! Sounds a lil' harsh, ay? However, it instilled a sense of a will to achieve a standard or position of achievement in whatever I put my hands and feet to. I was to do it until no more could be done and in such a way no other could do it. I was to leave my foot and finger prints everywhere I'd go!

Maybe I would not be the richest, but a print I would have left; a mark I would one day make. My presence would make a difference and the dash mark between my birth and death would not only matter but leave a substantial offering unto the world I once called home. The people I called brother and sister, mother and father, grandma and grandpa, friends, associates and acquaintances, a congregation at large, will have benefited by the mere inference that I was here. They will come to know Jesus, if I have it my way and that, I hung on his every

Word, as He hung on the cross for me. But excess in anything can be a dangerous antidote.

I have to say, this shelter taught me and my kids a bit of discipline, a bit of order, rules, schedules, housecleaning . . . which I had zero skill in, as well as divided chores and a genuine appreciation for life.. We could not even leave for work in the morning unless our chores were completed and checked off. Yard cleanup was twice a day and you'd stand in line to show how much trash you collected. Everything was on spotlight. There was no privacy except the lil' time you got in the bathroom. I'd take my cardboard box with my toiletries and supplies into the throne room, do what I had to do and come out in my allotted time because, you see, there were several of us in there. Mind you, drug abusers shared the throne room, as well. There was even a girl's pimp looking for one of them. My children had never heard that word, nor been exposed to that life. Little did I know, my turn couldn't be too far off in the near future.

Anywho, another of my grammas sayings, T.V. was off by 10:00 p.m. and lights out by 11:00 p.m. We even snuck our cat in because she had nowhere to go. We made sure to put her out before bed check when they'd come right in the rooms, no permission needed, with big ol' bright flashlights shown in our faces to do a head count ensuring that we had followed protocol. This was like clockwork, as some of the women were known to sneak out for many a reason, no need to mention. Yeah, this was altogether an experience in itself. However, I was thankful for a roof over our heads and although grateful, *I never want to return again.*

It still amazes me how we survived with little to nothing. What lessons were learned? I would not have met God in the same way or felt the sincere need for His presence in my life more than just being God. I needed and cherished a one-on-one relationship with Him that gave me the *power* I was searching for.

Shelter life was interesting. I took daily notes. I learned several lessons. One of the largest was the realization that I landed there like most due to an abuse of something. I felt that I was not a person, for shelter living and all of these women landed themselves there due to abuses of drug substance, "not me", over consumption of alcohol, "not me", prostitution, "not me"...

Well, one of the ladies asked me just what was I doing there in the first place, if I didn't have any addictions. I stuttered, then thought, and then stuttered some more, and then burst into tears. I think I cried every day for the first week we were in there. I didn't want to admit that I had a problem. I balled up, bottled up and shut down when they called for the AA meeting because that had nothing to do with me in my eyes. Hey! These people think I'm one of them. *Truthfully,* I was. I was a woman hurt, abused, taken advantage of and squandering money like I had no good sense. Why? What was my substance abuse? I'm a "good girl." I don't smoke, drink or cuss, I thought to myself. The AA meeting was a rude awakening to an experience I will never forget.

"Well something must have landed you here, baby girl. Would you like to talk about it?"

"Hi, my name is Jasmine."

"Hi Jasmine," I heard in unison.

I was at the lowest of the lowest. I never wanted my kids to see me like this. I was supposed to be their rock, not his, their backbone, not his, there ride or die lady, not his.

I am here because I put a man before me and my children. I have squandered our money. What was the difference? They squandered their money, too. Some of them on drugs, some on alcohol and yes, others like me, on men. I fit right in. I was blessed to have my children with me. Many of the ladies did not, until they'd gotten themselves together. Praise and worship would take place every night after the mess hall and then we'd go into service and AA. Days would pass by like the hands of a clock silently ticking away. I spent Mother's Day and my birthday in there. I'd call my boyfriend, but he stayed distant and quite busy. You ask, "Did he ever come visit me?" Umm . . . No.

My mind stayed consumed with whether or not he was seeing someone else or whether he thought of me. My birthday, just like this one, that just passed a couple of weeks ago, had gone by unacknowledged. There was a birthday of mine in which he actually saw me, asked me to braid his hair but did not realize it was my birthday. I never said a word. Though, I will never forget his birthday, my dad's or my children's fathers. It's just something you don't do. Or maybe I'm just being a "woman". My days would soon end there and the lessons mentioned above would be learned. Bonds would be created and another page would turn.

My son fell ill. His temperature skyrocketed and bumps covered his body, until he scratched blood from his skin. He then buckled his legs and dropped to his knees. He couldn't walk! I picked him up like a baby, began praying and rushed him to the hospital, where they ran test after test. It was God's way of getting me out of there, I felt. I refused to go back into that shelter living environment, as I was convinced he caught something there. I took him to a family member's house where he could lay and rest in the comfort of a real home. Shamefully, I had not told them where I had been living. That would not have sat well with them. Pride kicked in, as I tried to discuss hardships and possible living arrangements, in need of their help after screwing up my money. This was not easy but got us in the door.

What I had not said was that I was still in night school. Yes, working during the day and then attending night class a couple nights a week from 4:00 p.m. to 9:00 p.m., a requirement I had to fulfill in order to keep my job. I had not received permission necessarily to reside at my family's place, so I'd take my children to school and hide them in the lobby until one of the professors said, "Ma'am, are these your children?" I, being the only African-American student at the time in my class…, I guess they did belong to me.

I was shame that I didn't have a place for my children to go, but I had to finish this course to better support my children. At this point, I was forced to start leaving them in the car, checking on them periodically and making sure they were ok and not hungry. I'd come out and have lunch with them and then see them at the end of the night to tip toe back to my aunt's apartment by 10:00 p.m. just to sleep. I made sure to come in when all were sleep and leave before anyone awoke. I did not want them to even know we were there. A girlfriend of mine, my children know as T-T Chelle, took us in while we awaited our own place. I thank God for her and everyone else who stepped in during one of our many times of need.

God would soon bless and we would wind up in a four-bedroom, big beautiful house! Everyone, for the first time, had their own room. There was a nice backyard for the kids to play, two-car garage and we were on a cul-de-sac, so traffic was slow and the children could ride their bikes. Life was good but lonely. Once in the new home, I began to overload my life with time-consuming things. I had become accustomed to doing this. In this way, I would not have to acknowledge too much of the hurt, shame, embarrassment and loneliness I was feeling. Instead of filling it with the presence of God and immersing myself in His Word, I simply found things to do.

I enrolled back into school, taking close to $1,000 a month out of my pocket between tuition, gas, and babysitting. I found an overnight second job to make ends meet and on top of that, I was faced with yet another request to sign yet a second bond. Yes, this was for my heart throb. I was falling back in the hole. I was not able to take care of myself and my own children, but somehow I felt I had the ability to try to take care of others. I would house up to five families from that point forward. These families ranged from three to six people, some with dogs and yes, even guinea pigs! This was a heavy time for me. I wanted to help. Instead, I believe I severed several relationships. Thinking in some way we could all help eachother. Possibly, I would be able to collect rent for the room and rooms in which they resided. This did not always happen. My nerves got the best of me. I loved my friends, still to this day I do. I was afraid. I did not want to return to the shelter that I had just come from and was surely headed back to if I did not get a grip on things. I, sadly, was in no position to give help or support to anyone when my ability to help myself was coming from self and not God.

I had not yet totally received the fact that God was my ultimate provider. I was weak. I felt like I was sinking. I panicked and began throwing water overboard, animals and people too. I, to this day, have mixed emotions. I believe in God, but I am not God. There is a fine balance in understanding what you can do for someone and what God has set for them to do for themselves. Understand, I grew up with a muted voice. I continued to live out my entire life muted, never standing up for myself. I never really had a business sense, giving was much easier to me than receiving. I am uncomfortable asking for the things that I need and that are rightly deserving to me. This makes for a very good situation for others. However, there comes a point in which a house set to stand, requires order. Taxes are a real thing in the laws of the land that, biblically, we've always been instructed to follow. I have grown leaps and bounds in that time. I have come to understand right is right. We must work together to survive. Weight must be evenly carried, and shifted if both ends are to balance. Otherwise, one will fall. In many cases, the structure altogether will crash and burn and no one survives. It was important to me to stand and be the rock that I had not, up until then, been for my family.

My children have had to suffer and sacrifice because of my poor decision making skills and lack of wise budgeting sense. It was not fair to them that I continued in this manner. I grew tired watching myself struggle, working full time, while others not related to me were home all day, not contributing to the household. I was able to come home after work for but a moment before I went off to school, at times having no lunch to take with me because the food I purchased and cooked, was gone upon my arrival, eaten by those in the household but not of the household. Truly, "I thirst" as there was no water left either. My heart hurt so bad. I don't know what was worse, being hurt by a man or people that I thought were friends.

When I returned from school, I got the opportunity to kiss my babies and give them instructions for the night, as I was off to my overnight job. Any of this sound fair to you? On top of that, my neighbors, who knew my landlord, told her of all of the traffic in and out of my home. Yes, the landlord in which I had yet to pay rent to. You make this make sense for me, because I could not. I sat up all night watching other people's children at a group home, while mine were being watched by no one. Bills had to be paid, and all I knew was that my name was on them. No one else was responsible for them but me! I came to the point that with each family, I felt the weight was not evenly balanced and that I was given no tangible assurance that the situation would be balancing anytime soon. I gave move dates, well my landlord gave moving dates, and relationships were severed.

I had some of them leave, with no pay of any kind to me, not even to this day. Others demanded 30 day notices. Huh?

Yes, it got sticky. What started out as a kind act of the heart ended with broken relations and bad vibes. I still don't get it. Mad at me? I had my own troubles to work out and those could only be worked out by the grace of God. The same way I'm imagining there's would. My spirit was a bit shook, as all of this happened in such a short time frame, one after the other. My children and I never had the chance to enjoy the house to ourselves. I guess this go around wasn't that type of party.

I had work to do, as I was now getting myself together. My decision to sever the guest housing was confirmed as the right thing to do. It was a stopping ground for people to get back on their feet, while I continued to sink emotionally, spiritually and financially. I received a knock at the door shortly thereafter. I looked through the peephole. It was two policemen! My heart began to pound. I don't know why. I hadn't done anything wrong. Something about that police uniform does something to me, even though I was one. I opened the door and stepped out. "Can I help you?" I asked. They said, "Yes, we are looking for... who turned out to be a member of one of the families who stayed with us. Unbelievable! I had *no* idea some of the things that were going on. All I will say is that I am now ok with the decisions I have had to make.

Well, I don't know if I have a radar on me, or ham hock smelling perfume, but the one who possessed my heart in his hand would sure find me. Didn't hear from him much in the shelter, but now… He would show up to the door, duffle bag in hand and I would welcome him in wholeheartedly as I always did. Each time, believing it was genuine, for real and was going to work out this time. It wouldn't be long before I'd get that familiar call again.

This time I needed to contact more relatives, you see this was my introduction to the family, not family reunions barbecues, Thanksgiving dinners or a birthday or two. No. It was Hi, my name is Jasmine. # 1 enabler. Well, at least I'm sure that's who they saw me as having never seen me before at any of the above mentioned family functions. "He needs your help, I would say. Can you help us please? Yes, we we're in need of more bail money." I would then go into action with whatever funds I had collected and take care of business, towing cars back to my property, heading out to the jail to add money on his food card and taking in yet another doggy, "Daisy"

I know I was a police officer, but I was learning a whole new vernacular . . . can you say, commissary? I would retrieve his belongings, his wallet, cell phone and any other possessions he had on him at the time of incarceration. I felt so….. special. You thought I was going to say stupid huh? No. I felt so very important. I *felt* as if I had found my Boaz and I was his Ruth!

I didn't say I was healed. Actually, I was much less than whole. Yes, having his possessions put in my name for pick up gave me identity. I was his. He again, needed me. Oh, what I wouldn't do for *that man*. Entangled and locked in his snare, I'd go home and take care of all of his internal business including speaking to his probation officer. I was in need of major prayer and didn't know it. On one of the calls to the probation officer, I was asked, "Ma'am, do you know who you're dealing with?" It reminded me of the question G-Pa asked in the hospital…

"Has he ever hit you?"

"No!" I said to the officer, extremely baffled as to just who everyone was trying to make my guy out to be. I was very protective of him. That's how ride or die chicks are!

"Well, I am going to ask you to be careful because of his record," implying that something was wrong with my man! The nerve, *I thought to myself*. Ok. Clearly I am lost now. He is the most loving, gentle, tender hearted man I know, that is until he is angry. I didn't usually see the angry side of him unless he was arguing on the phone with someone else. It was never me. For the most part, he would leave and return when he was in better standings. But, that would soon change. He would shortly thereafter return to jail.

I allowed yet one more guest after my guy had gone. Again, the family outnumbered us and didn't stay too long. While cleaning the room upon their departure, I found drug

124

paraphernalia, small baggies and a weight scale for cocaine! Seriously? Amazing are the lessons I have learned, but all necessary.

God opened my eyes to much and allowed me to go through for such a time as this. I needed to lose before I could truly appreciate the gain. I don't look like what I've been through, but I've most definitely been a few places.

CHAPTER TEN

"That's Who . . . I Am!"

Ivisited G-Pa often in the hospital as I didn't have his son around with me. This is what I would do in my spare time aside from taking care of my children and, yes, another of his dogs left behind in this saga, "Dollar", who I later renamed to half of a dollar which equaled 50. Cents because he didn't quite have it all. G-Pa and I became close in these last days, as I would bring my boom box into the hospital or nursing home as he would periodically switch back and forth between facilities. I'd not only sing to him, but when he slept, I'd sing to the other patients in their rooms. They enjoyed it. I did too. I learned a lot from the people in there. I say last days because these would be G-Pa's last days here on earth. I, would in turn, be faced with another bail because G-Pa's life would come and go and he would never have had the chance to say good bye. I proceeded back to Aladdin Bail bonds to sign and he came home. This one he'd figure out how to pay somehow, but my name, nevertheless, was still tied to yet another bond. I didn't care. I loved this man and his father. We fed G-Pa, talked to him and helped to move his body around as he grew weaker and could no longer do this for himself. Sadly, the day would come where we all gathered around his bedside as the decision was made to remove the life support. He opened his eyes one last time, looked around at everyone and took his last breath. I had never seen that before in real life. I had only seen this on TV. To witness life evolve into death, was a transition I had yet to experience..

There were no other of the mothers of his children present in the room, just family and me. I don't know. I guess that made me feel as if I were family, too. G-Pa's daughter, my boyfriend's sister, began to sing, *I'll fly away*. I joined in with her and the room was filled with tears. How could I not feel bonded? My soul was tied, if not before, now for sure. G-Pa used to call me his Daughter-in-Law to all the nurses. That was big coming from him. I was indeed wanted. He gave me advice like a dad, too. I remember him questioning me in the beginning in regard to the validity of my position in his son's life. He had accepted me into the family, even requesting my presence before he passed through his sister. I am forever grateful for him and to him.

During those hospital visits of just he and I, we would talk about everything. I promised him that I would be by his son's side. I would take care of him. Even from the hospital bed, he would map out with me his future business plans. I was honored that he wanted me to be a part. He had many an idea and many a plan. The last one he shared was a mobile barbeque truck in which you could park and set out tables and chairs under an awning wherever you go. He wanted to call it G-Pa's Hot Dogs or G-Pa's Barb BQ, even naming it after my boyfriend, whom he loved so very much. I was tickled, but he was serious! I will miss those talks. I will miss him taking in my children. They were fond of him too! He often made them laugh. He even allowed my son to raise and lower his bed each time we visited the hospital, which he thought was the coolest thing ever . . . getting to use G-Pa's remote control, for the bed, that is; changing his TV. stations and sharing his meals I will miss him period.

With him gone, I felt there was no one to speak on my behalf. It was as if, at least to me, I no longer existed. I was now invisible and no one would know I ever had a legitimate place. The funeral for instance; my love got dressed at home with me. I helped to iron his clothes and braided his hair.

My mother called and sent him off with comforting words. However, I would be alone that day and that week. At the funeral parlor, he sat with his eldest child's mother. I sat in the distance. At the funeral, he rode in the funeral car with his daughter and her mother. I rode alone. At the funeral, he sat upfront with the family. Alongside him sat the mother of his eldest and at the funeral site, they all sat under the awning with the family. I stood on the dirt. I was there to support him and more so, I was there for G-Pa, who I know good and well would have told me to sit up front next to him if he could have. Tears flow to this day. I miss him more than words. He made me feel as though I mattered.

It wouldn't be long before the mundane routine of having a relationship would cause him to seek another. He tried to talk to me saying, "*Babe* I'm not who you think I am." I didn't understand or get it. I probably didn't want to get it, as I think back.

He continued, "You know those people who live across the street from us?" I shrugged.

"Yes," I replied.

"That's who . . . I am."

Who *you* are? *I thought to myself.* Beginning to put two-and-two together. Well, no sir, I was not accepting that because the people across the street were drug dealers with high traffic in and out of their home. I shook it off and acted as though he never said a word. Later, I found myself at work crying to a co-worker because something in the relationship didn't feel right, and things begin to rapidly spiral.

A training would take place at work in which I'd have to drive nearly 45 minutes to an hour to arrive there. I felt so alone trying to get back on my feet but feeling as if I was missing one step after another. My life was out of control and my inability to manage a dysfunctional relationship led me to a chaotic front.

Mindlessly driving, the rain splattered on my windshield. My wipers were turned on high speed and wildly thrashed left and right adding to the blurred vision I was creating in my life I would miss my exit altogether, as my mind and body were operating on auto pilot. When I came to, I would blink a couple of times before my chest started to move rapidly up and down. Panting, I began screaming to the top of my lungs. I was crying uncontrollably and sweating profusely. I . . . was at . . . the county jail? I had been so used to going there to drop off money or pick up items, including him, that my body subconsciously drove there. I was tired. I was no longer in control. What was I doing here? I was numb all over. Something had to give. I covered my face and cried out GOD HELP ME!!!!!... and even more songs would be birthed out of my experiences, my pain and my shame. Guide me oh Lord.... I am lost.

His Spirit Guiding Me

I walked out on the Ocean, so far I could not see.
The way back home, it seems so long,
I feel the waves consuming me
Oh…. Down on my knees I'm praying,

Father please rescue me.
A life without the hand of God,
is like a life tossed out to sea…
The waves of life, they are raging,

The waves I fight have no mercy,
Just when it seems all hope is gone,
I feel your Spirit guiding me….

Cry Out!

If you need God
To show up in this hour,
To give you strength and everlasting power,
Then open up your mouth,

Cuz, you must shout!

Your Father's business,
You must be about,
Cry Out!

The struggles real
There is no doubt about it
The Word of God we cannot live without it
Your walk, your talk, must live to represent,

So do not fear
His love is heaven sent
Cry Out!
The devil's job, it seeks us to devour,

It is our job to stand and never cower
Call unto Him Messiah from on high
In Him I live the old man he must die
Cry Out!

Trying to beat the stronghold of depression
Oh God my screams cry out in all directions
Stuck in a place I've never been before
Don't wanna be here, God there must be more!

Though I was blessed to write beautiful Lyrics, people who hurt you will never know how much. It just may kill them to feel the pain you felt. Let me take that back. I believe they live in that pain and, therefore, only know how to operate in that arena. I'm quite sure I have hurt my share of people, too. Again, hurting people hurt people. It is a vicious cycle that I now base my ministry around in hopes of healing one person at a time with the introduction of the true love of God.

The Plethora of my experiences: men, unhealthy relationships, agonizing fear, insecurity, unfulfilled talent/gifts, jobs, tasks, lack of self-worth, procrastination, financial mismanagement, child rearing, and church hurt, all caused me to be spiritually dysfunctional, leading to my disobedience and bed-ridden state.

Help Me . . . Somebody, Anybody!!! Wanting to scream at the top of my lungs and hide from life. Didn't know where to go or what to say, if anybody would care or if anyone believed in me and what I had to offer. I needed an open door not realizing, as my Bishop, Christopher C. Smith reminded me in one of his sermons, I was the door opener! I was too busy pretending to be something I was not! Who me? Yes . . . me.

I pulled the covers from over my head, decided to stop crying and because I couldn't pick up a large object and slam it against everything I saw, I took my dog out and ran until I could no longer feel my legs! Can you say numb?! Yes, this was the exact feeling I was trying to accomplish; to not feel any of the blood running through my body, a welcomed feeling at the time. I began to question my destination, as it had become too dark to travel any further. Though the posted sign above head said to leave dogs on the leash, I unleashed her, fell to my knees, and again began to cry. I cried like a baby, oblivious to my surroundings . . . God why? I asked. Though I'm not alone I feel so *lonely*! I was angry due to my now 39 years of poor decision making, to live a life behind closed doors, hurting so badly and down trodden, defeated, demoralized, humiliated, scared, anxious, doubtful and bound, no hope in sight, yet in public . . . Happy, overzealous, optimistic, surefooted, and of course, on top of it all. This was a double standard that was slowly, but surely, all of consuming me one event at a time. My soul was dying and I wasn't sure how long I would be able to keep this up. What would become of me? Could this be it? What would become of my children? Would this be the only example of living they'd be privy to? My God, My God, say it isn't so . . . Desperate for life, I began to fight!

WAR

It's time for war,
ain't playn' no more.
It's plain as black and white,
let's stand tonight,

It's time to fight,
it's time!
At the end of your rope, you can't see straight
The enemies knockin' at your gate

You cover your head, never leave your bed
Praying to God that the enemies fled
The devil's around to keep you bound
But the victories yours in this next round

It's time for war, ain't playn' no more
Let's set the score, the veil is tore
It's time for war!

Chapter Eleven

Close to the Fire

Even with all of the many lessons I've learned, accomplishments I've made and experiences I've had, I still have not arrived. As long as I live, I will be striving for the betterment of myself as a human being, a child of God, a mother, sister, daughter, friend and colleague…. But for now, I am simply at home. I have been here the last two days boxing with the enemy. I don't know why I fight Him knowing that it is in Him I win!

My birthday was June 1. Today Is June 3. In these last three days, I have been hit with not only rent due on the first, but also a storage unit notice that my things will be sold in a couple of days. My mailbox was full of bills. I also received a PG&E bill notice stating due to all of my payment arrangements having been broken, I must pay by, yes, my birthday or they will shut me off permanently until the full balance is paid. I, too, had a notice on the door that my daughter retrieved as we were coming home Friday evening stating my lease will be ending at the end of the month. We are sorry, but we will not be renewing your lease. You are obligated to pay until the end of your lease and must vacate in 30 days. Can this get better? Oh yes! It can!

Upon picking my son up from his new private Christian school, after pulling him from public school, which would be an entire other book in itself… In fact, he is currently helping me to write it. Be looking out for it entitled *"His Name is Cadence. He Beats to his Own Drum"*.

On the next morning, I get a visit by the new private school's principal at my car window as I pulled up to drop him off, stating I owed the school, of which a balance would need to be paid by when? Yes, June 1st, my birthday again, in order for him to return to school, in which he had only one week remaining until summer break. Well, you'd think having a job I'd be able to afford it, except I am not there because my son is *out of school* due to non-payment. I'm sure you know the game. Do we eat, have a place to sleep or obtain a decent education? You choose .Is that even possible in our society? I can't *even* cry anymore. Nothing will come out. I've been here before. This was considered a familiar place. When it rains, it pours, and then it storms!

W.C. began to stay out late at night and some nights not even come home. A co-worker asked who this person was that I was seeing? I gave her his name and her face transformed right before my very eyes from golden brown to white like a ghost.

"Jaz, I think he's a *pimp!*" Saying this with a look of fear in her eyes!

"Come on…get out of here!" I said. Shrugging off what she was implying and doubting the truth of what I'd heard.

That is a bit far-fetched don't you think? I would know that by now wouldn't I? *Wouldn't I? I thought to myself* . . . What in the world have I gotten myself and my children into?

I began to watch closely, listen a little more, read his Facebook postings, noticing days and times of the night he didn't spend at home. Things were beginning to add up: To what? . . . I didn't exactly know.

I read a post mentioning a bottom "B", a top "B", as well as a few additional terms I'd never heard of. I told my friend about my findings. She looked them up in the urban dictionary and just about fell out. I was in the game and didn't even know it. Random girls began calling my cell phone. I began to find hair strands, no lie, thay were not my length, texture or color. I even found female clothing that didn't belong to me. Eventually, I came home from work one day after leaving a $20.00 bill with him for gas money that morning only to find that he was gone, leaving behind only a note on my pillow along with the girl's number he'd be staying with if I needed to get in contact with him. He informed me that he loved me, but he'd rather use her money instead of mine because I have kids and it should be spent on them and not him. *Huh?* After 3 years of my life, time, money, heartaches....

In the Closet Hang his Clothes

In the closet hang his clothes
A story of their own I suppose
One would never know what they've gone through
A symbol of the struggles he once knew
Who'd of thought they'd find themselves here

From the closet they whisper in my ear
My dear my dear come closer don't fear
You may not know us but we've been here all year
We've come for a purpose not just to hang out
The dust we have gathered has a story to shout
You can't hear it due to your guilt and your shame
You believed anything to cover the pain

In the closet hang his clothes

Representing all seasons as he comes and he goes
Neatly hung awaiting his arrival
Laughing at this chick who's in such denial
If we could only speak we'd tell you the truth
The places we've been that keep you aloof

Come, come close, look at us and you'll see
The life that we live is not your reality
Wake up girl! Though it's cozy in here
The body we belong to is nowhere near

We don't mind, the downtimes cool really
Just hate to see you sad and looking so silly
Back and forth you walk everyday
We see you cry, we hear you pray
But look at us, even the seasons have changed
It's been a whole year and we've not been re-arranged

Everything sits where he left it in place
In its own little corner, in its own little space
You think he wants you? You think he'll be back?
He'll come when he wants, we stay on the rack

Lady we know, we've done this before
Some of our kin with the lady next door

Sorry, just kiddin' that wasn't so funny
But really lil' mama, wake up honey!
Waitn' like you in the closet we fit
We belong to him too and here we still sit
Even though were clothes we've been on a journey
On the run so much even we need an attorney!
It's tough for us so we feel for you
These clothes don't fit any man cuz any man won't do
At times we too feel that we've been replaced
Shirts, jerseys, jackets, jeans, shoes and shoelaces
We wonder too if there's been someone new
A girl? A Polo? …Or the latest new shoe?
We've been there for him so we know all you go through
Court, hospital, jail and even his school
We tried to make him look his best
Just doin' our job so he'd pass the test
Suited him up to gain his fame
Lights flashin', him dashin' at the football game
We were in court on his back days he felt so so low
Even sat by your side with your big hair and big bow

We heard you pray for him that was real nice
Then the judge read the verdict and the bail price
Back to the closet we go…
Won't need us where he may go…

But your heart was so kind and kind made you blind
Your faith in him bout took your mind
You then bailed him out and we jumped on his back
Not long after that, Pops had a heart attack

You helped to iron us so tender with care
Placing us on him, then doing his hair
You sat in the back, but we knew you were there
You always have been, you always did care
His tear drops stained us one by one
A day of pain and not very fun

Soon after we went on a wild-wild ride
Smoke saturated our threads a smell he couldn't hide
We were soiled and stained, ripped and shredded
Some nights didn't know just where we were headed
So here we are, together again
We go and we come, we always get in
You stare at us we watch you walk
Just thought it was time to have this lil' talk
While you cry, we sigh not knowing our fate
Both fragments and stagnant awaiting a date

Will... He... Stay??? Or is it too late?

Have we both been outgrown weathered and worn
Outdated, overrated, his heart always torn
Missing the old but loving the new

Surely there's more, we're just a few
Wonder if he knows to our hearts what's been done
If he cares how we feel when he goes on the run
The Bible says two can't walk less they walk as one...
His clothes I passed day in and day out
Never knew they had a story to get out
They wanted me to know, like a degree in college
My worth and my time would soon be acknowledged

To acknowledge me is to set me free
Like ashes and dust tossed out to sea
What I went through no one knows
Except in the closet...hung his clothes

We notice how you stroke us. As if we were alive
Your tender care and kindness helped us to survive
But it's not healthy you see, for we are not he
Soon you'll be used as ill, mentally
So wake up little lady that's what we're here for
To remind you in life there'll be so much more
Mission accomplished, we've done our job

Time to move on, now don't you sob

It's a new day, we'll all be ok
Go on with your life and pack us away
We know that you loved us, we know that you care
The memories we've made will always be there
Now in my closet there's an empty space
His clothes that once hung… have now been replaced

Every day since then, I reach back in my memory bank and try to piece things together. Often, I get little light bulb moments remembering times when girls would call me looking for him, or he'd come home all cut up and bloody. How close to the fire was I? But God… My days after that were pretty painful as you can imagine. I rocked and rolled in my bed, pillows drenched with water wondering what I did wrong. How I could have been better, why he left me? Where was he going that was so better than where he was? It was pure agony. I had been there for him through thick and thin, lost my work gun, my heart, my money, my soul, my house, my mind, my pride, my dignity, my everything but my kids. Meanwhile, he gained a degree from school, a new place, a job, a car and a new woman. Just didn't seem fair.

What's Fair?

Don't know what to do with these feelings
I'm feeling for you
Knowing it's not fair with all you're going through
Struggling to find my maturity,

Watching you handle things better than me,
I know it don't seem quite fair at all
Still I stare at my phone awaiting your call
It's not fair...

What you're going through
Don't seem fair but things will get better
Cuz He'll see you, through
Wondering why you're fighting our dealings

A gift from God's been given to you
A chance of a lifetime,
We both are deserving
Of a love that is true

Those tears that have fallen in long nights of prayer
The pain that you're feeling a pain we both share

Redeemed by the Master, His plan from above
Is peace everlasting, the peace of a dove

It's not fair…what you're going through
Don't seem fair…but things will get better
Cuz, He'll see you through
The time we were spending made this life worth living

The time that we shared, it showed me you cared
You made me complete, now I must retreat
Standin' in the background, I'm taking my seat
It's not fair………

Don't seem fair
Father, I don't know what to do
Your Word says that you know the desires of our hearts
So this one, this one, I'm bringing to you

Teach us patience Lord, as we come hurting on so many levels
We're tired, we're broken, some feeling like damaged goods
Abused, lost, deep in the woods
Remind us God that as we take communion

You paid the price to create this union
So when we think about what's really fair
May we be reminded it's your blood we all share
Back to the drawing board I go

Sittin' down in front of my little piano
I'll write a song that will heal
A song of redemption, if that's in Your will
Faithful I've been Lord, I've done all I can

I live for Your promise, for you I will stand
Holdin' to my Bible, I read what it says
I live on His Word because that's how I'm fed
My faith is abounding, my life on a tree

The fruit of the spirit abiding in me
Standing in the gap, you've been waiting on me
To open my eyes so that others can see
I trust in your name Lord, shout Jesus forever

Your right hand I'll sit at, my ultimate pleasure
You hung on the cross so that all men could see
Shed blood from your body, said it was for me
I live in the spirit now I must decree

Your faith is the measure of what life can be
Now look in the mirror, tell me what you see
A love that's unfailing, a love that's for me...
Try not to depend on the things that you've seen

Patiently wait on the Father to lean
His Word holds the blood that is covering
A love everlasting, no bondage you're free
His love has been given for you and for me

With You, I'll be bonded, your rib I will be
So trust in the Master, give it unto thee
And all that You're after
In Him it will be . . .

It's my responsibility, It's my duty
What You've instilled in me Lord
It's called integrity
More is required of thee in this society

Peace on earth good will to men
It's a priority
So what's fair . . . is that we do our part
For all He's done for us

We're His mold, His art
He's given us His heart
and a brand new start
So what's fair?

When you think about
What He went through
What He had to do to save us in lieu of
What He already knew

The sins, the faults of
 Both me and you
Sometimes I sit and stare
and think what's really fair?

Was it really fair?
Was it really fair?
So I'll live my life
Head held high, I'll be your wife

Til' that day comes, it's my sacrifice
I'll prepare, now that is fair
I'll be more aware and share
Your Words of redemption
Back to the drawing board I go …

Huh . . . how would I ever recover from this? Who could I tell? For I had been living in secret sin for a long time. The road was going to be tough. I still had parenting duties, work duties, ministry duties and night school. G-Pa was gone and W.C. was gone too, in an instant. Left all by myself! There's no one else to look to but God when all else fails. This is when the song I started a couple of years back could now be finished and birthed. Hence, *Praisn' All by Myself*. My first single. Can I say Glory be to God?!

Praisn' All by Myself

I live, I sleep, I cry, I pray,
I search for souls most every day and I,
Wonder why I suffer so,
I live for those who do not know,

You as the King, our Lord of lords,
A Gift, a God who opens doors…
How will I know if I should go?
The path you walked so long ago and you said

Believe in me and you will see
There is a place for me

And I know if there's a place for me
Surely there's a place for you

There was a time I feared His love
I looked to man not Him above
Confusion set on every hand
Building my house on sinking sand

I'm Praisn All by Myself...
Nowhere to go
Nowhere to turn
It was a painful lesson I had to learn

Saying yes Lord to Your word
Obedience is what I heard
Left by myself there's no one else
Look to God when all else fails...

But then, "*He*", appeared. The wind shifted again right back to a time when my heart was yet tender, and my flesh was in need of attention. As if you need to read about one more guy. . . *wait!* This is a good one. I thought. Let me show you how good! At one of my lowest points, I met another man! This was the only way I could foresee getting over the last one. He was a smooth talker if I had ever heard one. He was one of a kind. Let me tell you.

Truthfully, I wouldn't trade this experience for the world. In a twisted sort of sense, I believe this man loved me, too. I believe he wanted to be with me. I believe he meant every last one of the pipe dreams we shared. But I also believe that, sadly, he knew in the back of his head that he could never fulfill them, and *we* would never be together in that way.

I thought he was perfect. A sight to behold, a touch that sent chills up your spine, a word spoken that made you feel heaven even if for a moment because truly that's exactly what it was, a moment in time. I don't quite know how he did it, but ankle monitor and all, I still had my girlfriend planning a wedding to die for.

He and I had all of our colors picked out, guest list of invites, argued over our first song to be danced to during the reception, praise dancers ready to go, and get this, my pastor's approval. Oh, and my son called him *dad*...Yeah, that one! Just thinking back makes me ill. Even the people on the streets everywhere we went marveled at us. We were like the picture perfect couple; from the outside that is. It even felt like it truthfully from the inside. I believed everything this man said to me.

Upon getting off of his ankle monitor, He instantly moved in as planned. My real life had just begun. The one I had waited a lifetime for. I was finally with the man I would introduce to the world! It was on a Friday that he moved in. I brought him to church that same Sunday, three days later. I glowed as I paraded him around for all to see. This would be baptismal day for my son. A sacred occasion; one I chose to spend with him. He was surely to be the new head of our household.

We had dinner as a family after church. He drove my truck, and I paid. Oh, no big deal, just thought you may recognize some of my wonderful healthy patterns. We would return home after our family dinner, in which my teenage daughter scowled at him the entire time. It was as though she could sense something not good coming. She has always had that gift of discernment. I didn't wish to acknowledge it. I didn't want her to, get this, mess up my chances of finally having a man no matter what quality of life I was about to bestow upon my children. What was I doing? What was I thinking? Apparently, I was thinking of myself only. Was he even a good example for my son, considering the day I met him, he was dropping his prior girlfriend's children off to school? If you ever get me out of the twilight zone of a life I have created for myself, ... I tell you.

Upon arriving home, he immediately got out of the truck and began to chain smoke. Again, I heard the phrase that we were not . . . , basically, equally yoked. Huh? Now, you say this. I don't want to hear that! I'm getting married man! He requested to move back home. Yes, within 3 days (Friday to Sunday), I'd lost him. We began to move box by box, everything that we had moved out of his mother's home and into mine, back out of mine and proceeded to drive all the way back to *his mom*. I was mortified! As we've read in the Bible, a lot can happen in three days. What makes me any different?

I'd receive a call sometime shortly thereafter asking me if I would still be purchasing him "the car." We spoke of getting him a car, as he would have needed one to job search when he moved out here. Yes, I, too, was planning to spend my new tax money on that. You've got to know the answer to that one. Well, with all of my ill decisions, to this point, maybe not. I may have just hung up. Actually, I think it was on text. I would see this gentleman later, although nothing was ever the same. My trust again broken, my hope faded.

The last I'd ever deal with him would be the night he came out with his new car requesting to talk to me. He drove me from my town all the way to his. We stopped in front of a house, asked for $20.00, went to the house and returned, informing me he was popping a molly; something I had only seen on Facebook and YouTube. In fact, not too long prior, I viewed a clip of a man going nuts after having taken one. *Omg* . . . here we go!

Now I am in a car with someone who has just taken them, as well? Mind you, I am nowhere near home. I stared at him the entire way home thinking to myself, if I ever make it home safely I...I.... Oh never-mind. I am simply feeling degraded at this point. This is what he thought of me and my life. He carelessly intermingled my precious life with his frivolous ways? What about my children? What if those drugs had taken a different effect on him? Where would I be? Can someone say 9 lives? Clearly, he had little respect for me. Clearly, I had less for myself. When would this mindset end?

Later, he would phone in need of a favor. This was another of my weak moments that I justified as a "Christian" moment, knowing little of what it meant to be a true Christian. I ran to his aid or drove rather 40 minutes out to find that he had a young lady and her children in need of my help. A lady I had never met, seen or knew anything of. She had two of her three children with her at the time and was looking for a new start. She'd find "her new start" in me, as I agreed to take her in.

Introduced to me as a little sister of an old friend, I'd find out upon reaching my driveway, after a 40 minute drive back home, that she had actually met him on the internet and came to his hometown place after making good on advice he had given her in which he never thought she would take.. He, not expecting that would really happen, received the "shock of his life" when she showed up in town. Not being properly equipped to help her, he reached out to ··· (drum roll). . .*me*. What the what?!

156

But my past habits resurfaced like Jonah from the belly of the *big* fish, and out came my uncontrollable tendencies to enable. I took her in. All was well until I realized there was communication between the two of them during her stay in my home and none between he and myself. Hmmm? Amongst all other events, I could take little to no more. This episode would have to be chalked up and added to my many learning experiences. As life often does…It came full circle. She and I found a common bond and that common bond would only be found in God.

From Pimps to Preachers

From Pimps to Preachers
Musicians n' Lechers
Some that could have been keepers
If their feelings were deeper
I've been through it all, N' still I stand tall

Because of my call to help those that may fall
Fall for Jesus
Fall in love
Fall for the father, blessed from above

I Am the light!
I'll no longer be hidden
My faults are covered and my sins forgiven

Close to the Fire

So don't try and hide me so others can't see

The beautiful flower that my names meant to be
Jasmine, remember me?
Ride or die chick
But not invited to the picnic

Jasmine
Girlfriend at home
But at the church, sits alone
Jasmine

Your woman behind closed doors
But not out in the stores
Jasmine
There when you need

But don't dare birth that seed
Jasmine
Your love,
You made me share

Though me better not dare
Jasmine
With her for the creep

158

But home you must sleep

Jasmine
She prayed for you and stayed for you
Cried for you, 'bout died for you
She tried to do her best for you,

But still you could not see her through
She bugged you, but she loved you
She trusted you, then busted you
Fell to her knees and cussed at you!

She followed you 'til she couldn't do
No more for you
Her love was true
She thought you knew

A girl's gotta' do what a girl's gotta' do
Something new
So she fasted and fasted and now,
She is through!

She now lives for God
Yeah that's her new boo!
Some may wonder if this story is true
Look close at my scars

I went through it

For you!

DEGREES OF SEPARATION

In a world separated by degree
I see you and you see me
Though oceans apart parted like the Red Sea
We were ripped from the boat back in history
Me ripped from you and you from me
We've struggled to survive living separately

Now facing a world of hypocracy
Each tryna' fend with no democracy
Daily we fight the bureaucracy
Losing our souls just tryna' be

Now I find myself slippn' as a black woman
Lookn' for love wherever I can
Age...just a number and he's just my friend
He found in me something he believed in
Though living in sin killed my reputation

Now tryna' live by a church girl standard
Simply tryna stand though my names been slandered
Focus they said, girl focus can't you see?
There's a better way to your destiny
But feedn' my babies is all I can see
Drowning in the plight of independence, see
Dress to the ground now wearn' my crown
But the truth of the matter? There's no king around

So often I sit with an empty purse,
smurk on my face n' doubting my worth
Then along you came to set me free
Called me beautiful, funny and even sexy baby
Even though I'm a square you accepted me...

Who'd of thunk our worlds would connect musically
In a world separated by degrees
I saw you and you saw me

Planting a many seeds in the womb
Some will be nurtured, few will be groomed
Some will make it, some will be doomed
In a world separated by degree
I see you and you see me
Though in your arms I may never be
A part of your life ~ like family
Once a nightmare, now only a dream

I long to be near you walk beaches and parks
Stare in your eyes til' the skies get dark
Growing old with you's what I wanna' do
Have a nice lil house and a baby or two
Eat dinner at the table yeah that's what we'll do

But...instead I'm am here, and instead you are there
Instead we've been cheated of a love meant to share

You represent a world in the street
A world of pain overcoming defeat
When you look in the mirror and it looks back at you
It tells the story of what all you've been through
Lives lost, beaten backs!
Lives lost, heart attacks!
Lives lost, broken spirits!
Lives lost, I can hear it!
Screams of the mother's through songs they've sung
Screams from the belly, father's been hung
Who will lead now? Our ancestors gone!

Brings me now to our present day
Now understanding why you walk away
Now understanding why you say you can't stay
Looking back at me, your tears pay....

The cost of a way you could not make
The cost of the road you were made to take

So comfort you find in the streets where you grind
Through the billiards of smoke, the weed clears your mind
I'm in a house but I can't make rent
In the car is where your nights are spent
Why can't we agree to disagree, living as one in unity
When I see you, I see me
n' this ain't the way it's supposed to be
We've even lost the essence of our identity

As a woman I know I'll never truly understand
The pain of your struggle, the pain of a man
To provide for his family, show love and to please
Seemingly shattered, overcome by dis~ease
So, now as a woman I seek to relieve
My brother, my man, my king, YOU'RE MY KEYS!
See, keys' unlock and keys' get you in
Keys' in your hand are a sign that you win!
Keys in your hand are a sign of power
Take those keys black man and enter your tower
It's now your season, It's now your hour!

So come close my brother I wanna' comfort thee
Though my mamma and my daddy, they wouldn't agree
The church in itself is an entity
And the streets love no man, not...even.....me...
But YOU??? You I see, and you see me
Your dreams, goals and visions are safe with thee

I see you and you see me
Our worlds aren't as far as they used to be
I see you and you see me
Let's walk side by side into destiny
I see you and you see me

162

Together our power cancels misery
I see you and you see me
Our music over shadows our identity
I see you and you see me
Together our song will tell the whole story

Wish I could keep this moment frozen in time
Wish I could say that you'd only be mine
Wish our distance apart felt like only a line
Connecting my heart to yours and yours to mine
But the truth of the matter is ~ time moves on

So, I sit and I wait til' our next text date
Cuz in this day and age that's just how we relate
Time stands still, praying time will heal
The years of degrees that made us separate

You day, "I gotchu ma"... But do you really???
See your mind and your soul's what I need
ULTIMATELY
Our mind and our words have been so loaded n' so coded
Time to give our story back
To GOD~ The one who wrote it!

I still see you and you still see me
Together our song will tell the whole story
Together our song will tell the whole story
Together our song will tell the whole story...

Chapter Twelve

A Moment in Time

Feeling betrayed, I lived a stent of life that suggested I could care less. The things that had happened to me, I told myself I had to simply suck it up in order to survive. Wipe those tears away and get through this life the best way you can and if that meant others had to hurt, Oh well . . . It is what it is!

I would simply shut that part off figuring they would get through it just as I did. No one was safe at this point. I had sinned in every which way possible during this lifetime and had the audacity to pride myself in the fact that at least I hadn't killed anyone or engaged in inappropriate conduct with anyone's husband. Well, it depends upon what you consider "kill." I had aborted three children by this point and, yes, the stent of inappropriate engagements with a husband or two had ended. Of course, I subconsciously discounted it because one I was involved with flirtatiously prior and the other was on their way out of marriage. Nevertheless, legal papers were tied to the three strand chords and I was the fourth, which inherently didn't exist. I had no business, but in a sick sense, I believed I couldn't be hurt anymore, because these men did not belong to me in the first place. I was dead wrong . . . I believe I hurt worse. In both instances, I was in the end again *not* the chosen one. I would now face fear of one day being exposed.

I, a shame of a woman that was supposed to be so super holy, guilty for taking part in ruining a union that could possibly be mended, if not for my interference. The worry set in that because of this, no union I would ever have now would ever be blessed. What a mess! I had not only taken my soul down but had no concern for the man's soul that was involved either. I was all the way around out of line and completely out of the will of God. What would I do now? How could I ever fix this? Was it possible? Was there a way out or was it over for me?

"but God is faithful, who will not allow you to be tempted beyond what you are able, but with the temptation will also make the way of escape, that you may be able to bear it. (I Corinthians 10:13b)

My sister would come to stay with me for a while, as she was in transition, too. This was my sister in Christ, experienced, educated, and full of the *Holy Ghost!* This would prove quite uncomfortable for me, as this was a woman I highly looked up to. Was she heaven sent or what?

In this time, I allowed my Mister Wonderful to come back one more time… I know, I know, but this is my journey. This is my truth. I, for the first time…, was exposed. This caused me to have to face myself in a manner I really didn't want to have to do. She was able to see the inside of my life and it wasn't quite like it looked from the outside, of course. I was so embarrassed, but so entangled, that I didn't have the courage to separate the two lives.

Slowly, I believe, due to her interceding on my behalf, warring in the other room, praying in tongues and table talks she would have with me in between her speaking engagements, she'd tell me how much I had going for myself, what she saw in the spirit. She brought to my attention how powerful I was and/or could be in the kingdom. She was there to awake me to who I was. I believe for such a time as "that", she was assigned to me. I began to wake up, but froze before I put her words into action. My flesh got the best of me. I applied not one principle of the Bible and like Peter, I *looked down.*

I was afraid I would not be able to pay bills, even though the blessing of the power of God was being downloaded to me by her on a daily basis. What better compensation can you ask for? This was the genuine love of God being downloaded into my spirit. These were seeds that were sure to harvest if I was patient and mature enough to allow them to. I was not. I wanted to do things my way. I wasn't finished living my life the way I wanted to. Do you hear that? I, I and *my, my*…. Where was God in that? Where was my faith? Where was my loyalty? Where was my ministry? Still trying to find myself, I wasn't willing to extend the stay. Didn't matter, soon after, my boyfriend would leave, too, and we would be facing homelessness again. Wait! Was I still calling him boyfriend? You'd think I would've learned by now. But oh . . . no, rock bottom hit me right smack dab in the face, as I sat in the lobby of the welfare office with my *big yellow packet* in hand indicating to all that I was in need of a handout. I was trying my hardest to be discrete, because I am a school teacher right?

Many of those in town that I communed with on a daily basis were also in here. I sat frigid with my head down, so not to make eye contact with anyone. How did I end up here? Angry, I tell you! I had to put on a soft demeanor, as my son played on the floor and in the seat next to me. He, not able to sit still to save his life, began to ask question after question.

"Where are we mommy? What is this place? How long are we going to be here? Hey, Mommy! There is so and so! May I go and give her a hug???"

"No!" I tugged, "sit down, sit still and be quiet! It will only be another minute." I believe it was 8:00 a.m. We didn't leave until nearly 5:00 p.m. He huffed and puffed, but soon went back to playing in his own world; a world I wished like anything I could be in on that day. The loud speaker would come on shouting . . . "Jasmine Strange to Window A!" Oh my dear Lord! Humiliated . . . that I was in this dilemma in the first place! Seemed I couldn't get up there fast enough, as they called out again "Jasmine Strange to Window . . ." OK! OK! Could they please stop calling my name, I thought. When calling my name was exactly what I needed someone to do. See me. Hear me. Help me. Acknowledge me. Love me.

On my way to the window, I walked past heads held low, matted hair, tear filled eyes, ripped clothing, children with no shoes and dirt smudged faces; my heart *sunk*. There were pregnant women both mature and teenagers. Men with canes and wheelchairs, some in vet outfits also filled the isles. There were those in suits and ties with looks on their faces of wishing this could be any place but the place they were in. I could feel the dismay in that office, a nightmare that wouldn't end quick enough. There were babies crying and other children running and playing tag, totally oblivious to where they were and what was exactly going on.

This, to them, was simply another errand in the life journey of their parent that they were being dragged along to, not realizing this was how they would be surviving the next couple of days, months or even years. For some, this will be but a moment in time. For others, this will be a lifetime experience.

Either way, I did not want to be there, although grateful to God to have a place to go in my time of despair and need. Stares glared at me as I approached the window almost as to say . . . what in the heck are you doing here? What's your story? We are in much greater need than you. Me, all dolled up and finally in high heels, purse and cell phone in hand instead of my ball cap and sneakers. Many of the amenities that some were not privy to on a regular basis, as "Obama phones", as they called them, were not yet out. But I, for once in a lifetime, regardless of the reason, was most definitely in need. The lady at the counter greeted me with a piercing stare that made me feel even more ashamed. This had become so routine to her that, unfortunately, there was no light in her eyes either, and she took what was left of the light out of mine. Her voice was monotone and after a moment of awkward silence, she finally said yes?

That's it? "Yes?"

Heart pounding I said, "uh uh...," stammering a bit over my words. Wishing to God she could just feel my pain, read my mind and this could be over without me having to open my mouth. But this would not be the case. It seemed the entire room got quiet as to listen to what was about to exit my lips. I looked around to see who was looking and where they were in relation to the conversation I was about to have (Approximation is something to be mindful of at all times).

I waited and tried to pick the right moment to speak. You could tell the lady at the counter was getting pretty agitated with me. She may have even expressed it verbally.

"Ma'am, can we help you?" She blurted out sounding like a foghorn sounding off!

Here goes. I just rushed it out of my mouth. "I need help. I have to be out of my home *asap* and I have two kids. My PG&E is to be cut off today and I have no food. I am unemployed and housing says they cannot help because I have no job. See, I was laid off and . . . !"

"Stop," she said . . . raising a document in her right hand in the air. "Fill this out and we will call you to get back in line."

"Back in line," *I thought to myself* . . . Imagine the embarrassment of it all. Some of you reading know just what I'm talking about. I took a deep breath, as I moved from one line to the next . . . feeling like I, along with the others in line with me, were being herded like cattle, only to be told by the last window I approached to come back on an appointed day and time. The process seemed as if it would never end. I did leave, however, with a voucher for a hotel until I could get myself and my children into our next place of adventure, this time sneaking our dog into the hotel and leaving the cat behind in the neighborhood until we could come back for her.

I received a letter in the mail shortly thereafter requiring me to come to a class that was to help teach me how to, in so many words, "become a more responsible person". This was a stipulation in order to receive benefits. In other words, if I was to have help from them, I'd have to attend. So, attend is exactly what I did. Let me tell you; It was on the list of the most demeaning things I've ever had to do. I could teach the class, I thought in my mind. I had a real hard time. *Pride* was definitely getting the best of me but, moreover, as a Believer in God, I knew this was only temporary. I was a believer that things are not as they appear. I had vision. I just needed a little help to get over the hump. I did not need to be told how to dress or how to land a job. I just needed a little help to get over the hump.

However, in all things we learn. I realized, just like in my shelter experience, I was there for much more than what the teacher had to say to me. I had to dig deep and understand who I was and whose I was. This way I wouldn't be so offended each time they talked down to me. I had advisors in this program who said I "am not" and "could not" to being an advisor who says, you can do all things through Christ Jesus! Do you know they would only help me with a teacher's aide resume, even though I had already been a teacher for years, amongst all other career fields I've listed in this book. They told me I just had to get a job, any job, even if it was only but a few dollars an hour.

Huh? Forgive me, but . . . I have two children to take care of, including myself. I believe I am worth more than that! I had a girl in class tell me I didn't have any problems, as she began to tell me hers. I explained to her that I don't look like what I've been through, nor what I'm going through. It is my intention to appear as God has called me to appear...be who God has called me to be, have what God has promised me to have! In between that time, I fought like a dog for justice! After standing at the front door of my home, back against the wall, listening to my landlord saying,

"Sorry honey, I don't know what to tell you, but you're going to have to go."

I remember looking to the heavens as she continued to ramble, asking God to help me! I knew not of what to do at this point. I heard Him say, "Be still and know that I am God. I will help you, but you must wipe your face and believe. Trust that I can and I will."

Like a flood, revelation came to me like never before. I was no longer afraid. I didn't have that panic struck fear I used to feel every time the doorbell rang knowing it was my landlord and not having what it was she was requesting of me. I had even fallen so far as to tell the children to say mommy was sleep, in the shower or not here altogether when she'd arrive. For once, I stood strong in the face of adversity. I stopped taking *no* for an answer.

I was not receiving unemployment even though I was laid off due to a downsize in our student population of no fault of my own. Unemployment said I was being penalized 6 weeks for an overpayment years ago. I had just accepted it and went into the hole! I felt pressed on every side . . .

We are hard-pressed on every side, yet not crushed; we are perplexed, but not in despair. (2 Corinthians. 4:8a)

I began to *listen* to the voice of God. Digging deep down inside, I spent my days, instead of crying, writing letters of appeal left and right! I even wrote to Illinois forgetting I taught there and had invested in money there, that I would never receive unless I worked for them a total of 5 years. So, I requested to cash it in.

I wrote to housing and appealed with my situation. The man was on his last day headed out of the country and said, "Ma'am because I hear your situation, if you can show me proof of income unemployment or other, I will reconsider your application for rental assistance." I received a letter in the mail as a reply to my request for an unemployment hearing. I went. Due to a simple oversight in paper work, my case was reversed! I won! Subsequently, I got my job back, too! God is great! I followed this same principle with my education.

You see, during this year of downfall, there were several causes. I wish I had learned to operate in this matter or mindset earlier on. I was struggling, trying to make ends meet because I had, even after years of schooling and test after test, still not received my full California teaching credential due to transferring from teaching in the state of Illinois. I paid out of the nose and repaid in many ways, not only financially, but my time and lack of time to rear my children, as there was a period of time that I worked overnight shifts at a group home just to make ends meet. I allowed house guests that changed our lives in many ways both helpful and some not so helpful, but even in this, God's will prevailed.

And we know that all things work together for good to those who love God, to those who are the called according to His purpose.
(Romans 8:28)

I finally decided to take my mother's advice that has proven to be quite helpful in my latter years. She told me I had done enough experientially as well as educationally to have acquired my credential by now. I prayed, then picked up the phone and called San Francisco State University. They made an appointment for me to come down, meet with them and have my transcripts and work experience evaluated. They looked at me puzzled and said, "Ma'am, you have everything you need.

What are you waiting on?" Tears filled my eyes. They said you simply need to take and pass the RICA Test, and we can send off for your Teaching Credential! Look at God. I tell you. This was only the beginning to what God can and is about to do in my life. How about yours? This book is not so much for me, as I know my story, but prayerfully for you. I don't know exactly what point you are at right now in your life ...

But as it is written: "Eye has not seen, nor ear heard, nor have entered into the heart of man The things which God has prepared for those who love Him." (I Corinthians 2:9)

It is time for you to start trusting God and get ready for the miraculous. Do you believe? Can you conceive? If we can believe, all things are possible. Belief in action will move the hand of God. My daughter, Lyric, was now in need of a Tenor Saxophone and a band uniform which included a pair of boots equivalent to the cost of a month's electric bill alone. This was all for a trip to London. The SAX cost $1400, the uniform $200, and the trip $3,000! Regardless how difficult the task appeared, I was going to get it done! I had a history in sports and creating game plans, but this time God was the Coach! The game plan was strategic in nature to use my voice for His glory!

People said, *No You Can't...* You haven't even paid rent yet, tell your daughter sorry, but maybe another time. Times are hard right now. She'll just have to understand. I listened for but a second and then carried on. Again, I prayed.

I wrote letters requesting help, I Facebooked my friends and Lyric's supporters. She and I sang at churches. I even sang in the BART stations with my little hand painted sign, folder, can, and boom box. Guess what? She went to London. Later she was chosen to study abroad in the Dominican Republic with an organization called Global Glimpse. This time she went on scholarship! Cadence, subsequently, was accepted into The Grammy winning Pacific Boys Choir Academy, that travels the nations. He, too, received a substantial scholarship! Investment in your children pays off! Stop letting peoples' no's stop you from living.

What then shall we say to these things? If God is for us, who can be against us? (Romans 8:31)

Cadence is actually on a trip to the Opera House today with the San Francisco Boys' Choir. I sit in a Starbucks in San Francisco, awaiting his return. I am so excited to hear about my boy's adventure. A man of the alternative lifestyle sits next to me as I type and begins to converse with me about life and just how far we've come as a people all together. It really wasn't so much about black or white, gay or straight, but the fact that your life is a story. He told me his. I was in awe of where he had come from and the value systems that he had. He spoke of Robin Williams' passing and that no amount of money could buy your freedom but that you must be free from within, making the life that you want for yourself.

He spoke of making a house a home and how many have monetary things but no true place to call home. Inner peace is truly priceless. Our views may be different and sins not the same, but boy did he hit on something right there. I desire my children to be free, free from bondage and the mindset that they "are not "able due to the absence of monetary provision, but that their money comes from an endless source in their Father God and Savior Jesus Christ.

I started today off not knowing how I was going to get Cadence here today. My aunt was so gracious as to pay for his summer camp, however, travel remained at $30.00 per day to San Francisco and back for the both of us between Bart, bus and cab. The Bible says do not worry about tomorrow. It will take care of itself. Biting my nails, I chose to believe. I even gave my sandwich away to a homeless man and chalked today up to fasting, having no money for myself to eat. It hurt my heart to see people without, regardless of what I was experiencing at the time. He was hungry and it was the least that I could do.

Our travel fair would indeed be covered that summer and his camp uninterrupted!

"35 for I was hungry and you gave Me food; I was thirsty and you gave Me drink; I was a stranger and you took Me in; 36 I was naked and you clothed Me; I was sick and you visited Me; I was in prison and you came to Me.' (Matthew 25:35-36)

CHAPTER THIRTEEN

Now, this is Living!

I Came home on yesterday and there was a check in the mail. Although small, it covered my next day. God you're amazing!

If He did it before, He can do it again! He's the same God right now, the same God back then, as Tye Tribbett radically declares in the lyrics of one of his songs. I cannot attend the type of ministry I attend, eat the fattening food received there week after week, learn the Word of God the way I have been taught, witness the miracles I've witnessed, live the life I am living, breathe the air I am breathing and wearing the body of armor He has given me to wear and not believe that He will take care of me and my children as he has always done.

I have been young, and now am old; Yet I have not seen the righteous forsaken, nor his descendants begging bread. (Psalms 37:25)

How much more will He do for me as I am living in, under and by His Word now than He did for me when I was still living in sin? I shall hold my head up high and declare the power of the Lord is covering me like *never* before. I will *live* and not *die*! I stand in agreement with you at this time facing similar situations that the devil has no authority in this matter. Through God, you have all power! The resources of wealth and riches flow in and from your belly. Be awakened to your call and walk in it, for it is that very thing that will *make* you free!

I declare all power will manifest itself in every work of the Lord that you put your hands to. Where there is depression, it be no more! Where you are weak, you are now strong! Where you once embodied the spirit of fear, you are now fearless! Your body is your temple and in it will live the Spirit of Christ, who will strengthen, nurture, comfort and heal your soul like never before!

I encourage you on this day to not only know Him but to invite Him into your life wholeheartedly. *In Him, you cannot fail! In Him, you cannot fail!In Him, you, cannot fail!* Hallelujah!

If you are not in a church home or do not have the proper ministerial covering, I urge you to go to your local parishioner and seek fellowship with the body of Christ. It is important to be connected, to be able to seek guidance, prayer and simply fellowship with like-minded saints. Your strength will come in the bond between you, your Lord and your fellow body.

You will have an accountability like never before. You will also be accounted for. At this moment, if you never have done this before, seek God. Ask Him to show His face, to reveal Himself to you. Ask Him to come into your heart and take up residence. You want Him to dwell in you and walk with you. There's no better feeling in the world in times like this than to know that I can bury my head in His bosom, seeking answers, and Divine direction in His name as *I* step back and watch miracles unwrap like gifts before my very eyes. You know the saying…Don't knock it until you try it. The world has failed me many times over, but The Lord, My Lord and Savior Jesus Christ; The Light of my life, and the Light of the World *never* has.

No ma'am . . . No Sir, I do not know what tomorrow holds, but I do know who holds my tomorrow and with that, I am not afraid. I am actually excited! I purposely throw the enemy off, in that he desires that we break, weaken, bend, crack, sift ourselves like wheat and blow away, leaving only that which the spirit desires as useful to the kingdom.

The plan of the enemy is that we perish, but the *promise* of God is that we have everlasting life. I know you may or may not have already heard this a million times but maybe, just maybe, my obedience in writing this a million and one times may just be what it took to accomplish the mission. If so, so be it; if not, it's the truth anyway. It is my prayer that you are blessed abundantly, that you receive life over death on this day and forever more. It is my prayer that you know there is *nothing* too big for God, the creator of *all* things. I have been at the highest of highs rubbing shoulders with the big wigs and in this same lifetime, the lowest of lows with those that couldn't see the light if they were the ones carrying the lantern. In all of those cases, God was there. He was present and took care of me by teaching, guiding, caring, scolding and molding me, that I may be able to speak of His good name as I am doing now.

Believe me, I never imagined in a million years, at least in my lifetime, that I'd be writing a book. Me? Are you kidding? Let alone release a CD. And with that said, I believe this is just the beginning. I welcome those failures, those dry, desolate and despairing times, for it, once again, was the cumulative assignment of each step that has brought me to this very moment in time, this moment that I am now sharing with you. May your eyes be opened, your mind be shifted, your voice be heard and your life forever blessed.

Today I sit atop a mound of dirt, not in an office, nor at a desktop. Although this will eventually be a typed up, copy written and printed, document, I am at present moment with pen and paper found in the back of my trunk hidden in between the crevices of remains from my storage that never quite made it into the now 1 bedroom apartment during my newest transitional period. On one of my early morning jogs, after dropping both of my children off to school, I paused to take a brief moment to get in tuned to, in line and on one accord with the Spirit of God, who covers and keeps my soul. I did this in a form of lying down and meditating, as advised by my aunts at a round table meeting the night before. I was already in a fasting mode and had been now for at least a couple of weeks. After about a 30-minute span of lying in a prone position (face down that is) moment with the earth, communing with my Father. I arose hearing many things from the Lord. I would have stayed longer but for the barking dog snapping me out of my ever so serine state alerting me that his boss, the Pittsburg PD Canine unit, was checking to see if I was ok, alive and still kicking.

Once I sat straight up, an indication that I was, in fact, ok, the policeman drove away in an effort to allude to the fact he had other pressing obligations besides his concern for me. I looked straight ahead and there was a large sign in front of my face flashing *slow down*. The next signage I saw said to *check your speed limit* . . . Amazing, as that was the very first thing mentioned in the opening message my Bishop would give at church the following Sunday. You cannot tell me the Holy Spirit is not working right now, even as I type to confess and testify to you at this moment. I had felt guilty up until this point, as I felt being busy equaled production.

I had felt like a bum this entire year for being unemployed, either sitting at Starbucks all day, writing another song, another page in this book or sleeping until it was time to pick up the kids. Eventually, I began to fill my days with things, such as recording my CD material, posing in photo shoots, reading the word of God and most recently jogging to clear my mind and restore not only my body but my soul. Of course, the enemy loves to play tricks with our minds. That is where the enemy operates best; in our minds, that is. He wanted to make me feel as though my time at Starbucks was useless, jogging wasn't going to do me any good, there's no way you can take the weight off, let alone clear your mind.

He made me feel stupid for taking pictures because who am I kidding, I'm not a model I told myself, even though one of the pictures I took in that time happens to be the cover of this book. I had no idea! Thank you Jim Payton, at *Through God's Eye Photography*. The enemy also made me feel as though my time had been wasted writing my songs, when I could have been doing something else. But something like what? However, my confirmation had been delivered . . . Not an ounce of His

186

precious time had I wasted in this season! In fact, I was right on target; more on target than I had ever been in my life thus far.

What I did today counts! What I am doing right now counts! It will be the song I write today that will save and/or heal a soul tomorrow, get this, not only tomorrow but years from now when I am no longer here. It is my responsibility to deposit deep into the future my gift to the world, as I have received so many, some who may be reading and from those who have gone on before me. Clarity was needed from God to be able to receive instruction from the Master. This time would prove to afford me the ability to get the clarity I needed to do what I am called to do to fulfill my purpose here on earth and to save a soul from totally consuming itself. It would be this time that would graciously do this for me. I stopped questioning it and began to receive it, believe it and act on it.

My mile run now completed, as the dog continues to gallop, paying no mind to the fact that I have begun a new project. Her venture and mine, totally different but equally important to the flow of life . . . *lol!* The Lord has spoken and it is now time to sit and write. I am amongst a large green field. There are several man planted logs that the prairie dogs run through, however, there are no jungle gyms and no swings.

As I stated at the top of the chapter: just myself, paper and pen atop a mound of dirt. Now, this is living!

This, is what He'd have me to write on this day: It is not our physical state of being that drives us, though it plays a large role in the fluidity of this thing called life. A life can be well lived by properly maintaining how it feeds the soul. With having said that, feeding the soul is what, in turn, gives life. It is an innate desire for the human body to live. To thrive, conscious or not, the body will fight to the death for life! Our mind and our soul is what gets consumed and causes us to do the unnatural. If you cover your mouth and nose with your hand, eventually you will remove it, for the body will fight for its own life despite your mental state. If you sink under the water placed in a tub, you, too, will pop up in due time. This is why we do the unthinkable and resort to means of permanency by way of guns, drugs, alcohol, hanging, jumping from bridges or in front of trains, even subconsciously unprotected sex. It takes away the body's natural means of defense.

These are things we know we will not be able to come back from. For we know if we gave the body a chance, the mind an inkling of room to choose, it would fight, call on the Master, and choose life over death. Our biggest battle, as Joyce Meyers has written about, is truly in the mind. It is not physical at all. These are simply houses that we live in here on earth but it is the mind and soul, that is alive and fighting to survive.

We are all given an amount of time here on earth. Though the length of time is unknown, it's what we do with it and in it that is most relevant. Don't be so mindful as to if someone likes it or not. The goal is not to simply exist, but to thrive, enduring all factors and relying on the strength and power of the Holy One. Then, passing on the blessing of life yet unto another soul that it might not be consumed as well. Hallelujah! This is what we call sharing the good news of the Gospel of Jesus Christ and all that He's done for you, for me. For us! Life is found in the blood of Jesus Christ!

For the life of the flesh is in the blood, and the blood speaks. Leviticus 17:11

CHAPTER FOURTEEN

Can You Hear Me Now?

Our voice is wrapped in our DNA, but I never knew I'd find my voice in something as simple as a pen and paper. I'd been told for years that I didn't have one; a voice that is, whether it was direct or indirect verbals. I was told to speak up or sing louder. My voice was not favored because it spoke in a whisper. It was soft and could not be heard by man. What do they call that? Inaudible? Is it man that I need to hear me or God?

The deaf communicate quite eloquently and get their messages and points across quite well, I must say. Their senses are more in tuned to the person as they must focus on them even the more to understand. They are felt by way of vibration, expression, facial and intense body gestures. Their eyes then become the window to the soul and their heart captured in the intensity of their delivery. It is not something that had to be screamed or turned up, rather paid more attention to. When you want to know something, you will. When you wish to hear something, you will align yourself with the author, the singer, the teacher, the dancer, the actor, the preacher, artist, in other words, the deliverer. The closer you get, the louder you will hear their heart, their message, even if only in the spirit. It is the message and not the volume that counts.

I had been told on occasion that my voice was weak and had no signature. Not realizing *voice* is a form of communication; the reception of one from another. It is the outcome of what leaves one's soul and enters another's. It was never said that it had to attain a particular volume. If the message goes through and is received, it has been successfully transmitted. I was told that if I were singing from another room, no one would know who I was. To that I say, it is not me that they need to know but the Father I serve. I want them to know, hear, see, and feel God, not me. The word "voice" is not only defined by sound but is used as a verb for expression, articulation, declaration, to reveal, announce and or publicize. It is to get a point across and as we know, there are many ways to do this both in volume and the lack thereof, hence "silent treatment". Yes, you have a voice. It is your choice how you choose to use it to get His message through.

It is a trick of the enemy to *silence* you altogether. Thank God for the Holy Spirit sent to intervene. Though my voice is soft and gentle, it screams the loudest with this lead pencil in my hand in which I'm currently using prior to the computer and on to the press, which is my ultimate goal. If you are reading this, *I made it! Can you hear me now?* It has made it to print, confirmation of something whispered, even silently spoken. You are now witness to my voice. Whether it is liked, approved or not, it is heard and has now reached the masses. That's pretty loud, if you ask me.

So you tell me how real this is when currently I am sitting in Barnes and Nobles on Feb 1st, 2014, without even enough money to purchase a cup of coffee, let alone pay my rent this month. By the time this book comes out, coffee will be on me! Now, I'm shouting!

Today, May 2014, we lost one of the world's *"Greats"*, an inspiration to women, to the black community, and to mankind, at large; to writers and to a nation that could not always speak for itself; whose voice could not be heard. Prolific! Today, my book has been confirmed. This is what the news reports repeatedly said about this woman, that she was prolific. Defined from the inside out, this is what she was...

"There is no greater agony than bearing an untold story inside of you." –Maya Angelou

As one goes, one always steps in. Little did I realize the magnitude of this moment...for such a time as this. Maya and I? Never imagining in my wildest dreams that I'd be stepping in after Maya Angelou. No matter my magnitude, I am now putting my foot forward and following through on my untold story, my muted voice. I am working toward fulfilling that prolific status, that the world may be touched, as well, by a word written even if not spoken, it shall be heard. How timely could this possibly be? A sign? A wonder? A miracle? For me?

For I know the plans I have for you," declares the Lord, *"plans to prosper you and not to harm you, plans to give you hope and a future.* Jeremiah 29:11

I'm remembering the very day my mother phoned me while I was away at college, states away, just to inform me that Nikki Giovanni was to be on my campus that day.

The educationally astute woman that my mother is alone should have caused me not to be shocked that she'd have more knowledge than I of what was taking place on my campus. She had done this before with Princess Diana, the Queen of England and even President Obama, whom at the time was Senator.

Unfortunately, I don't know how serious I took her at 18 plus years of age, and missed all but Mrs. Giovanni's visit.

I ran down to the forum where she'd be speaking on that day, fought through the crowds and pressed my way to the front, even though I hadn't the slightest idea the depth at the time of who she was. My mother made it clear that there be a sense of urgency placed in my efforts to be there on that day. I was, and what a magnificent experience it was. Having no idea what impact it would have on my life today, I am forever grateful. In pen and paper, I have found my voice.

I've often thought how easy it would be to write a book. I'd just simply use all the scripture I could find and attach them to all of the many negative experiences I've had in my lifetime. Now wouldn't that be just so easy? Packed full of juicy detail, an easy read for all to feel sorry for me. Don't get me wrong, I've done that and there's a lot to be learned from it. The testimony is real, as many of you live it daily. However, the Lord spoke to me saying, "Why give the enemy all of the focus and attention? What does he deserve for all of the grief he has caused?"

The world has promoted his story far too long. It is time for this generation to rise and exalt the name Our Lord and Savior Jesus Christ, the One who has come to save us from ourselves. The Almighty, all powerful, all knowing, all wise, love of my life, Healer of my soul. Our souls shall not be consumed.

We shall live by His stripes and in His name, the Word of God will be declared and live on throughout eternity in us.

He asked me from this day forward to lift Him up in every way possible. When I get ready to give any attention to the enemy, I think of His glory. This book is a promotion of all of the good He has done in my life and the good He can do in yours. It is a gift He has given to us by way of a choice we must make; Eternal life or eternal death? It is as simple as mind over matter.

How awesome it is to have the control over your mind, maybe not your situation, but how you choose to process it, what you chose to believe and whom you choose to give the power and control to. In all of these things the control is directed back unto you when given back to Him. It is quite powerful when you think about it. I am aware that I cannot control all of my situational experiences, but I am empowered by the knowledge that I am in control still yet of the well-being of my mind, body and soul. As of today, begin to take back the power of your life! Naked you came and naked you shall go. It is the relationship with God that is your ultimate concern in this lifetime and what matters most. Your present state is temporary when you think about it but your soul is eternal and well worth the fight!

CHAPTER FIFTEEN

Cocoon to Full Bloom!

There came a time when I had to make some pretty level headed clear cut decisions. It was important that I made them in a state of clarity and not emotional distraught. What would be the best path for my life at this point in time; not what would be best for others, but for me. I had to use discretion in this season of my life like never before. I had been hurt so bad that the only way I knew of protecting myself from it was to not care. I didn't care about borders.

I didn't care about boundaries because people had crossed mine so many times, it didn't seem to matter to have them or not. I did whatever I wanted, whenever I wanted. I wasn't under the covering of a church anymore and didn't answer to anyone, let alone follow the principles of God. Sure, I was nice and kind, but I didn't take heed to any governing rules in my life. I followed man.

I continued to sing for God, professing His name and good works, but I was no example of Him, so what good was all of that? I came to a point where I was running myself ragged. I was experiencing defeat on every hand, not understanding why? I was spiritual and I was singing songs of Zion. So why was everything failing around me? I had lost my home, mate, car, job, even my driver's license. Why was I feeling defeat and no power? Why was I not effective in the earth realm? Why could I not pray my way out? There were decisions I had made and still had to make.

It is said when you desire to make a change, you must make an effort to put forth significantly. This means a change in life habits, life styles, life choices. Sure, I am grown, but grown doesn't mean what we do is best or best for us. We have to realize what we do also has a great affect and impact on our children and those in our immediate surrounding and takes away from the impact we could have at large. It reminds me of the movie "Back to the Future", where each choice, decision and action made by "Marty", could have detrimentally altered his future and very existence.

Much of what I was doing was running around in circles being busy. I had no particular route, plan of action, or destination necessarily. I couldn't be on a time guide to gauge whether or not I was on target when there was no destination nor best route chosen. I was aimlessly moving about this earth following the lead of others. Downright *lazy* as I think of it now. I made no effort to go to God in prayer and ask what His vision was for me. I simply followed the visions of others. Although it is good to support the visions of others, I strongly believe that God has a plan for us all.

For I know the thoughts that I think toward you, says the Lord, thoughts of peace and not of evil, to give you a future and a hope. (Jeremiah 29:11)

If we are so caught up in only fulfilling the vision of others without taking into consideration our own God-given vision, we lose sight, and thirst not, for what He has called us to do, as well. Again, balance is necessary.

My season of discretion caused me to take a look at several dynamics in my life to see if they were truly working together for the good. They were not.

My place of dwelling changed and my locational address was not given to all. There would be *no* keys given out to anybody! No dating would take place in the home. In fact, I didn't need male company in there at all. For what? I began to monitor my food intake and eating habits. Fresh fruits, vegetables and water added. I began to do my hair, add a small portion of make-up. My aunt gave me a bunch of her clothes, many still with tags. Dresses even; I put them on, paraded them around, took pictures in them and downright began to feel good about myself again. I chose to seek God and His spirit to guide me and not man. I found a church home closer to my newest residence, where I could fellowship with the body of Christ, be used in my gifts and callings and expand my wings to grow that I might fly and soar in the directions that The Father would have me to. I was able to seek wise counsel by entering into a place of covering. It provided me security and stood as a defense to the rough winds of the world.

Again, I found shelter and could now focus my attention and ear to the Lord and that which He originally called, designed and purposed me to. No longer did I allow people to choose my way for me, but rather I chose to use the leading of the Holy Spirit and its discretion.

I accepted fewer engagements, or rather used my discretion in which ones I would attend. I made sure they were things that made me smile. I made sure to involve myself in the things that made my children smile. If it was a drain on my spirit, my children's spirit, or not in line with the spirit of God, I wanted no part of it, and I prayed about every engagement. It is a must that we pray. Prayer is our way of communicating with our Heavenly Father.

Understand that speaking with those that are down here on earth is wonderful, but there is little anyone here on earth can do for you in comparison to what God can do. The magnitude of help most of us are in need of cannot be fulfilled by the man alone. I did pray. However, when I prayed, it was one way only. I asked, asked, asked. I did not, however, stop to take the time to listen and thank Him. I was so busy downloading all of my problems that I failed to leave room for the answers, or guided instruction, much like my children as they come to me with their issues and tears. As I try to enlighten them on how small their problem really is because mommy has been there before, and I know exactly what to tell them to get through it, their cries and shouts are so loud that they can't and don't hear me. I say to them all of the time, "You asked me the question, but you won't allow me to answer. Do you want to know or not? Would you like my help or not?"

Their tears dry up long enough to look me in my eyes. I wrap them in my arms, cuddle them and begin to tell them it will be ok. Then, I give them the answer. You see they came to the right place. They knew the source that would empower them, but they weren't listening. Aren't we much like that?

I have made a conscious decision to *stop* following man and allow His Spirit to guide me. He is my source in which I gain much power. Things began to look up for me. The answers He already had. I am now choosing to listen. There are principles the good Lord left for us to follow and abide by. They are in the Bible. Everything you have, you had at birth . . .

Before I found you in the womb I knew you, before you were born, I set you apart; I appointed you as a prophet to the nations. (Jeremiah 1:5)

I did not realize it was all located within. I had yet to realize who God created me to be. I was not able to find myself even though I was a worship leader. I could tell others about having a relationship with God but, at this point in my life, I was lost. Sad, I know. Again, it reminds me of Robin Williams passing. He was able to make the world laugh but ever so sad inside. It was obvious to me that reuniting with the church was crucial. I needed to heal and become rooted and grounded.

I began to explore the God that lived inside of me. I began to hear Him speak *to me*! I picked up the pen and paper, dusted off my laptop that I had purchased some years back for unknown purposes, as I am what my children would call computer illiterate, and began to express myself like only He could through me. I opened my mouth and began to record. I opened my mind and expounded on my faith, trusting that God would supply all of my needs and would help me to support not only the visions inside my belly, but those birthed into my children, as well. When it's of God, He will make a way. My Bishop Christopher C. Smith, always says.

"God loves to glorify Himself! A way is being made right now! Glory be unto His Holy name."

I recall attending a leadership meeting led by my Bishop. During the course of the meeting, I asked the protocol for setting time constraints, limits and/or deadlines as it pertains to ministry. What he said next was key.

"Daughter, you cannot put God on a time frame. He does not operate in our time. You must wait! Wait on the Lord for his perfect timing. Continue in the works that you are doing and, surely, He will let you know when the timing is right."

Ministry is ever going. There is no "I've arrived" moment. There are steps, stages and levels, but we will continue to grow until the end. The following morning during service, he went on to say that it is dangerous when the leader proclaims a stop in his or her personal growth. If the leader stops growing…, we all stop growing. This would be the year I'd release my EP CD, and my plus size, mid-age modeling photos to the world! This would be my ministry finally moving forward, for now that is.

I was anxious and in this 40th year of life, pressing myself harder and faster than I had ever done before. It was like I had a point to prove. I began to lose perspective on the goal that one might come to be saved and know Christ, to give his or her life over to Him. I began to place time constraints on everything. I'd say I'm going too fast or too slow. I'd say things like, "When I come off of this fast, the CD will be released!" When that didn't happen I'd say, "Ok, well, instead of the CD being released, I will release the single by this date." When that didn't happen, I found myself confused and discombobulated, as nothing seemed to be working out the way I'd planned.

Well, those dates are in the past. Moving forward, I will plan for the single to be released before my birthday! Oh, by the way, today is my birthday. Got to love it! I felt this had to be released while I was still 40 or…or…or… I didn't have a choice. I was moving so fast, I never stopped to consult the Lord. Lord as I type, bless this book even the words already written, typed, read or spoken. God, it is in your timeframe that I desire all things to take place. It is in your time that this book be completed. It is your hand that I desire to be upon each page and your breath, I desire to be breathed into each word. It is your Word, your message, your promise I wish to be heard. It is your will I wish to be done. Give us our bread, our daily bread, knowing that tomorrow, surely, will take care of itself.

I wanted things to move so badly and so quickly that I forgot to consult the Lord. Is that not what we do? Then, we have the audacity to ask Him, why? I can hear God now, like I would say as a parent, "Because I said so, that's why." There's a reason why God does the things He does and in the timeframe that he does them. Thus, the message the very next day at church delivered by the Bishop just a day after I had asked Him of the time limits in ministry.

He spoke on the butterfly's process of life, cocoon to full bloom, and why things cannot take place faster, nor can each stage proceed another. A caterpillar must sustain the pressure placed against it as it squeezes out of its cocoon in order to strengthen the wings that will allow it flight.

He went on to explain how man should not try to help the caterpillar out of its cocoon, as it would surely suffer. It is necessary that it is given the opportunity to fulfill each stage of development on its own. I am beginning to understand a bit more. My struggle is most definitely strengthening my wings. In God's time, all will fair out the way it is supposed to. So I say to you…wait on the process. Don't be discouraged. Understand when your wings have to become a little stronger to withstand the travel, especially, if where you are going is of great altitude or distance requiring uncommon stamina and endurance!

CHAPTER SIXTEEN

Starve it Out!

"PERMISSION TO BE YOU"

It is important that you give yourself permission to be you

Tell yourself and others' it's ok to be true to you

It's ok to think the way you think and walk the way you do

So look like you, talk like you and cry the way you cry

It's ok to be yourself even though no one understands why

You are the only one who can represent your trail

And let me tell you my love, you do it all quite well

No one can tell your story nor express your creative mold

It's done so very meticulously, through the powerful tools you hold

Now claim who you are, then walk in it

There's no one like you on this whole planet

No one can say who God's called you to be

You are simply you and you's ok with me and thee!

It is important that you give yourself permission to be *you*! Tell yourself it is okay to be you! It is okay to think the way you do. It is okay to walk like you walk, look like you look, talk like you talk, write what you feel, smile as you trot, even if no one understands why. You are the only one who can represent you, and let me tell you, you do it well! No one can tell your story. Self-expression is one of the most powerful tools you hold. Claim who you are and then walk in it! I like that phrase: "Naked I came and Naked I will go." No one on the planet earth made you, nor do they have say so in whom God called you to be. *You are simply who you are.* And that's okay with thee!

There will be times when you need to hear clearly from God. The world, even some believers, tends to clog up our ears, dull our senses, and cloud our vision. It is not, by any means, easy out here, nor is it expected to be. The goal is that we would lean on and depend upon the Lord for every direction and every instruction, that the things accomplished in this life be that of His will and not that of our own. To do this takes quite an abundance of discipline, understanding, willingness, and obedience.

Sometimes, you just have to get quiet and still. Not the most fun place to be, I get it. Ask any child and they will confer. Lol. Who wants to be quiet, let alone still? It's so quiet over here, let me tell you! But for this book, I'd lose my mind! Wow. But for this book: A book designed to heal a soul on its way to consumption. A book designed to equip one with the power, knowledge, tools and sources to fight; A book that is my living testimony; A book that I could never write amongst the horrendous turmoil, procrastination, clutter and confusion in my mind and life. Those that know me well understand and, most undoubtedly, would agree.

I cried last night. I cried because although I am *not* alone, I was lonely. You understand where I am coming from? I desired the touch of a man, the caress of his hands, the warmth of his body next to mine, the gaze of his eyes into mine, the very knowledge that he was present. Only he was not. He, whoever that is, has not been for quite some time now. In fact, while taking the trash out, one of my 'favorite friends' (well that was the only title I was given, even though we had engaged in things not designed for friends) passed by in his vehicle with another female friend and waved, as if I were the neighborhood mail carrier or what have you. With fake smiles and waves of hands, we exchanged a cordial but uncomfortable, "Hello, how are you? I am fine, thank you, and yourself?" as they drove off.

My heart sank into my shoes and again, because of course, I was soul tied to this man as well. I felt every bit of grievance imaginable. Why her and not me? It all started to creep back into my psyche, as you know the fight is a daily battle and as one of my students would say to me daily, "Ms. Strange, the struggle is real." Boy is it ever. Have you ever cried from the inside out? I was hurt. I took my dog out for a walk and sat in the park, as my body cried for at least a half hour before the tears ever began to flow. My muscles in my sides and stomach aching as they constricted with each whimper I tried to hold back. Why could no man see that I was valid material for a mate? I began to ask God. Wait?......... Was I? Oh, I don't know! That is not the point. I *was alone,* still, *now at 41*! My focus still not where it should be, which was on God and God's business. Oh how I desired to be like Ruth, where I was so focused on The Lord that Boaz would come right up to me! That's what I called him you know..."My Boaz". Still single, I felt it unfair that I never even got a first shot at it! A relationship that is..., a real one. I eventually dusted myself off, walked back home and continued to cry until I fell asleep.

Morning would come and my eyes puffy and swollen would tell the story of many tear-stained nights. Only this one was different. It didn't linger on and on. I felt it, but yet and still, I understood it. I understood its purpose, whether I liked it or not. It was necessary. It would prove itself necessary and valid in order to complete the task set before me by God.

This book needed to be completed and would not, and could not, in a state of comfort, cuddling and cupcaking, as the kids say, wrapped up in someone's arms that would never be my husband anyway. What is the point in all that? It was time for Kingdom business. It was time to begin the process of what God had called me to do. I didn't realize it, but I intentionally cut myself from these gentleman one-by-one, taking the keys back from my home, moving out from another home, changing my phone number, not giving out my new address, putting myself on a dating website and then taking myself right back off, and stopping phone calls made to a man that I found ever so irresistible, knowing even if for one more night of romance, which I would just adore, it would never progress any further than that, as he was still getting to know me after 2 years of dating and yes, sex. I didn't say I had totally been delivered yet. Even dating within the church proved itself fatal. I'd lose more time, money, dignity and self-worth.

I would always be a friend. So I chose to exit, even though the offer remained on the table to do the friend with benefits thing. I wanted more. He made it clear there would be no more at this time. I had to gather some strength and source of discipline from somewhere to not be comfortable with that situation. I may not be his idea of a wife or life partner, and I may not be altogether ready myself, but deep down, I knew I was worth more than that. I believe you are too! If I can be nothing more than an example of healing through self-love and acceptance, I will be. Now that's a reputation I can live with. That's a word I don't mind being called, an *"Example"*.

This is a form of fasting ladies and gentlemen, when you intentionally deprive yourself of something your flesh would otherwise desire, for the greater good. This is when God can really talk to you, when you can really hear from Him. This is when your purpose becomes clear and things begin to line up. The world is loud and busy. It is fast-paced and has mercy for no one. There are times when you simply, as the old folks used to say, *steal away*. We need to pull back from the world and those things that consume our mind, our thoughts, our fleshly desires, our wants over our needs and our needs over someone else's wants. When we begin to override others' welfare and well-being (our children or the congregations we serve, possibly) to please our own, we need to step back and re-visit our true purpose. It is the ability to push back from things that empowers us to do the great, the unthinkable. This enables us to carry out the will of God which, in turn, gives us life!

Fasting can come in the form of many things. But it must be *a sacrifice*! I would love to call that man, write him a note, even show up at his door, but no! Some of you may desire a double cheeseburger with bacon, extra mayo and fries, but you've decided to tell yourself no! There are many other desires you can list, as we all have our week points. You know yours. This is not the time to judge. This is the time to identify what that thing is that is taking up the mental capacity in your mind, the healthy space in your body or is eating at your soul, and come up against it! We must starve it out! Dehydrate it! Detoxify so that our bodies will be healthy and strong enough to fight in this next round. The next round will require all of your well-being, your strength, your will power, your focus, your heart, your compassion, stamina, and a clear mind to complete its assignment. It is for such a time as this that you will go through your temporary wilderness. It is quiet over here…. The phone doesn't ring. The invitations have stopped. Don't fret! You will make it! You will come out on the other side of this thing! You will be victorious! You can obtain favor that will follow your fasting! It is written in His Word! Nehemiah spent several days fasting and praying before he asked for and received favor.

When I did not live according to the Word of God, and I was outside the will of God, I lived a life of paranoia. I was forever looking over my shoulder to see who was there. I felt like people could see right through my soul and had to constantly wonder what all they knew, if anything at all. Looking someone in the eye was not a favorable thing for me to do. I lived in anguish, stomach in knots, not desiring to pick up the phone, in which I'd have to answer any tough questions. Truth be told . . ., I was probably in this alone. However, sin ate at me alive daily. It was the most uncomfortable state-of-mind to ever have to be in or experience. I felt like the whole world knew my story and I'd be exposed at any minute.

This is a life I am positive many, unfortunately, share because we try to straddle the fence and live a daytime/nighttime life combined. If you haven't noticed by now or yet...*It doesn't work*! This lifestyle surely will consume your soul faster than any of the above-mentioned hardships. Listen. There is a peace that surpasses all understanding. There is a peace that is promised to you.

Be anxious for nothing, but in everything by prayer and supplication, with thanksgiving, let your requests be made known to God; 7and the peace of God, which surpasses all understanding, will guard your hearts and minds through Christ Jesus. Philippians 4:6-7

It can happen in this lifetime. It can happen overnight. In fact, it can happen now! Stop for a minute and say this with me....

Lord Jesus, forgive me of all my sins. I believe that you died on the cross, and on the third day God the Father, raised you from the dead. Right now, Lord Jesus, I open the door to my heart, and I received You into my heart; as my personal Lord and Savior.

Thank you, Lord Jesus for coming into my heart.

Now, allow me to share what has just taken place and how, because of the words *you* just spoke into the atmosphere, your life will be changed forever. The Lord and Savior Jesus Christ has been received into your soul. He has been given permission by you to sit on the throne of your heart and at the head of your life! There is no one greater that can do the things He has done for you and is getting ready to do for you! Get ready for signs, miracles and wonders to take place in your life!

You are free to shed your old ways. Your flesh no longer can weigh you down and no longer has power, control or authority over your life. You are in the hands of God. You are in the bosom of Abba Father. There is no peace to be found like the peace of God. He stands in front of you like a shield of protection from the enemy, from the world. Though it exists, it cannot hurt you the way it has in the past. Your mind is renewed and your ways of thinking shifted. Therefore, when the storms come…and they will, you know it's working for your good. I don't know about you, but I can certainly find peace in that.

Where you are, He will be always. Finally, *peace*! In your darkest hours, He will provide light. *Peace.* When all else says no, He will say yes! *Peace.* When the world begins to crumble, you will stand. *Peace.* When there seems like no way, He will make a way. *Peace*...comes from knowing Him and knowing who you are in Him. But what happens when we turn back from His *Peace*?

Turning back affects everyone that is a part of us and the generation(s) that are before us. It is equivalent to massive destruction on steroids leaving no survivors. The masses that would hear will now not. The masses that would see will now not. The masses that would know may now not. The masses that could have shared: now cannot. When you realize that this is so much larger than you, you can begin to respect and reverence the magnitude of it, as well. God has called us forward. He is calling us Higher. He is not a God that would lead you backward.

Funny; the things I write on, I tend to go to church and my Bishop will be teaching on the very topic. Has that ever happened to you?. This was confirmation for me that the Holy Spirit was alive and kicking! I was headed in the right direction. Even If you are not quite there, it's good to know you are on the right path. He spoke to this same topic and mentioned how detrimental going back is, as well. He prefaced it with the very fact that going back after leading one to Christ sends a message on confusion. It not only weakens you, but the entire body of Christ.

I view it like going back on *your word*. You know how you view individuals that have gone back on the promises they have made or the guarantees they have promised. You may have had me once, but why should I buy something you don't even endorse? It sets our team back and gives way to the devil.

Confusion does set in and doubt begins to consume the minds of those that were already on the fence, let alone anyone who was already on board or even those who may have considered being enlightened for the first time. When they see our own people can't stay connected and engaged, it makes the world look that much better. The proof is in the pudding and as they say, "Show me the money!" People want to see the life we talk about; what the life following Christ provides.. The favor you say God has for those who follow him.

Your wavering and/or failed attempt to remain steadfast once you know the truth can also adversely affect your children and your children's children. I believe this is one of the things that caught me the most. It is one thing to damage myself and reap the consequences, but to watch my children endure and suffer the wrath is an altogether different ballgame.

Not only is your reputation on the line, but your ability to possess power, the power that will be needed to sustain the one and only life you will be given here on earth. It is an out of body experience I am feeling as I write in this chapter. I feel strongly about our being and our being here. It is something to fight for. Life. Since God is life, it is His name and His Word we want to keep alive. It is our life source. Going back is instantaneous death. Even though you will be living, you will be as the walking dead. I would rather die to live.

I was so afraid of life and the gift God gave me that I would not show up to events where I was scheduled to sing. I would claim sickness or prior scheduled children's engagements or whatever excuse I could come up with. I continually spoke all kinds of negative situations into my life. I am not sick; I am well! I have all power, all knowledge, all understanding and all ability through Christ who strengthens me! Philippians 4:13

Ahhh….my personal awakening! How I now see my vision as it is viewed in God's Eye. I have a responsibility to move forward in His Word. For me to turn back now would place doubt back into the minds of those that converted because of me, place fear back into the minds of those that thought I really and truly believed in the Word of God. It would cause many to waiver in their newly found belief and create a panic or complete shutdown to someone who finally had hope. It would be yet another abortion of life. This time the life would be a spiritual one that would affect many.

Being the change that I want to see requires action! I am challenging myself to take action in the change I want to see. I wish to encourage you to do the same. We are the only ones who, through Jesus Christ, have the power to change our current situation. Now, how powerful is that?

After reading several books, attending seminar after seminar, and listening to all kinds of self-help tapes, even throwing myself before the altar at church, having hands laid upon me and crying myself into swollen eyes and a head full of ache, pulling out any last remaining hairs from my lashes and brows, I'd determined that none of it mattered unless I began to put all that I had heard, seen, felt, believed, and learned into action. So, *I got up*! Yesterday is *gone*! *Hello Tomorrow*!

I lay prone upon the floor yet again at the altar at church after a routine praise team rehearsal turned into a full blown worship service. (I love when the Holy Spirit takes over and we are blessed with ministers of music who listen and adhere to it.) Our Praise and Worship leader, Minister Dasha Moore, went one by one and prayed for the entire team! However, I was out of it…, already slain in the spirit. I began to feel someone kicking the bottom of my feet. I moved over a bit, thinking it was someone who needed to get by, though I was still sprawled on the floor face down. The kicking grew more intense.

I thought to myself…, "Why is this person kicking me?" Then I hear a voice over the microphone. It was the voice of Minister Dasha prophetically shouting, "Woman of God! The Lord told me to tell you to *get up!* There is much for you to do!" I got up and ran for my life! Screaming and crying. All I can say is I'm glad the doors of the church were closed. Otherwise, I would've been running straight out of those doors and onto the streets of Oakland where rehearsal had taken place on that particular evening. I didn't care what I looked like! I knew it was the voice of God! I responded and I ran!

You see, just prior to that I had lost my grandmother, my mother's mother. The news came to me as I was exiting the courtroom in Pittsburg, California, after receiving news that I would be evicted in the next two weeks! I sat in my car, hands clasping my head in disbelief, ignoring the phone calls of my job wanting to know when I'd be returning to work for that day; the very last concern I had in that very moment. Fear set in as, once again, I knew I'd now lost the matriarch of our family, the comfort of having living ancestry that you could always fall back on and knowing I would now be once again facing the possibility of my children and I being on the street. How could this be? I was working! Still in, yet I was not making enough money alone to pay rent, car cost, electric, garbage, food, children's school expenses, rental insurance and storage (because the one-bedroom apartment my children and I resided in couldn't possibly fit the items consumed prior in the four bedroom home we had just lost.) I couldn't sleep. This couldn't be real. People only get evicted after 3 to 6 months of non-payment right?

Not 3 weeks! What was going on? Our complex just received new management and wanted to up the rent $200 per month. I was the last unit in which had not gone up yet. This would be the easiest way to clean house and start again, as my contract did not permit me to have to go up just yet. The lawyer for the apartment building called me out of the courtroom on the date of determination to get me to sign documents stating that I would agree to pay within two weeks; an amount I just couldn't. He said we could settle out of court and I said whew! Ok! However, when I walked away, he walked back into the court building.

Upon calling our case number, I was no longer there and counted as a no show. The lawyer said that I had signed an agreement to pay. Of course, I couldn't pay the amount he was requesting in the time he was requesting it, but thinking it would buy my family and I some time, I agreed to sign. My nights then were filled with anguish and nightmares. I jumped every time the door would be knocked upon, thinking each knock was the sheriff. I hid, not believing this was happening. It was all a bad, bad dream. The final night had come and I was to be out by 6:00 a.m. that next morning or expect a visit from the sheriff. All I could envision was a man with a large gold shiny badge and big cowboy hat pointing me out and down the stairs with all of the neighbors watching. I had never seen anything like that before, yet, this is what I imagined and dreaded happening to me in front of my children.

A girlfriend said I could come to her home and rent from her for a couple of weeks. I did just that! I thank God for friends who was there to help me in the daytime hours move large items out of the apartment and into storage that I just could not foresee doing by myself. Up all night frantically throwing things out of my apartment and smashing others into storage, even bringing some to the back of my classroom, an embarrassing venture in itself. It was an out of body experience! Pouring rain, I stuffed my kids and dog into the car, again leaving my cat in the neighborhood. Yes, we eventually got her and she's with us to this day. However, upon arriving at my girlfriend's home, I lost my dog as she jumped out of the car and ran off. We eventually found her in a local shelter, moved out and into Motel 6, taking cabs to school and work, as ol' faithful broke down yet again.

We would, in this season, go from place to place staying with an aunt here and there until we could get someone to trust renting to us after an unfair eviction being placed on my record. Being an actress as well, simultaneously, I was cast in a play in the City of San Francisco at The African-American Shakespeare Theatre Company. It was the world premiere of XTIGONE, an inner city spin off of Antigone, written by Nambi E. Kelley and directed by Rhodessa Jones. My son, being at all of my rehearsals, was cast also. This would be the saving grace in this season. It kept our minds off of the inconceivable and allowed us to appreciate life in quite a different manner.

CHAPTER
SEVENTEEN

Prepped, Primed and Purposed . . .

I am still here! We were uncommonly graced and placed into a beautiful three-bedroom with a large backyard and friendly neighborhood. The kids could again ride their bikes and have friends over to play. The dogs were now able to run freely in the backyard and we could now sing around the piano again that had been in storage for the last three years of our lives. To know that tomorrow trumps today gives hope to any situation. As long as we're given and continue to receive the blessings of opened eyes, breath in our bodies, and another day, we should use it to seek out to accomplish what God intended our lives to be. Funny how my thoughts and even my actions have been so trained to believe that what I do every day punching in on a clock for a paycheck is what makes and/or defines who I am. Actually, my purpose becomes fulfilled as I release my inner man to serve those things required of me here on earth. In doing these things, I find my true and authentic self; what I used to label as my hobbies. We've given way to a call of man and not our calling by God. Hidden behind man's work, many of us are dead inside and, so, long to "Live Again" (yet another single I have recently written). Many of us desire to live for the very first time. What has God called you to do? Stop and write it down. It is ok if there are multiple things. It is equally ok if there is just one.

Sometimes, we count ourselves out because we believe there is a limit to our gifts. For instance, we believe that we all get one or no more than three. Your gifts are unlimited! It is the capacity of your mind that you limit. God has skilled you to do a plethora of things even though one may stand out over the other.

After writing them down, you may notice that they all go together or line up in some fashion. Now, take those things and see how each of those could benefit the kingdom of God and His people. Once you've determined that, begin to write out a plan of action, even if you don't stick with it, as it may change over and over amongst the course of time. Ask yourself . . . Do these things bring you joy? Can you see light in these things?

Will the kingdom benefit from your presentation of it? What would be the effects of never presenting it at all? Has this material been presented before? Is there a way you can present it like no one ever has?

Begin to get excited about life. Begin to see it all over from a new perspective. Begin to see it and live in it. Get excited about His Good works!

Let your light so shine before men, that they may see your good works and glorify your Father in heaven. (Matthew 5:16)

May your light so shine. This is the start of your new life! Every day seek God. Ask Him for direction in your ministry. Ask Him what things should be worked on today. Each day will bring with it new mercies. Remember to follow as He instructs you, as it will be vital to your success in it. Continue in His business while you wait on Him. He is here and He will show Himself to you!

Through the Lord's mercies we are not consumed, Because His compassions fail not. 23 They are new every morning; Great is Your faithfulness. (Lamentations 3:22-23)

Each day will be an adventure. Each day you will learn and see something you didn't the day before, each day will begin to close the gaps between what was broken and what is now healed.... Not only that, but the exciting part is being used by God. He will now use you, as you have proven to be a willing vessel as He embarks on healing another life of which you now will be a part of due to your commitment to this walk and your fight for your life. It is your fight that will ultimately save another. This is what we do in ministry. One soul at a time, and *your soul* is worth fighting for! You will live and not die! You were designed to be a well-oiled operating, functioning creation! You are of the most powerful designs on the planet earth.

I recently attended a women's group at my church in which they were teaching from Cindy Trim's book, *The 40 Day Soul Fast*. It was day one, introductory day and I, again, hadn't decided whether I would speak that night or not. Do I want to go around in a circle and share all my problems and weaknesses and start up the water works in front of everybody? I'm on the Praise and Worship team, designed to lead people into the holy of holies! I am supposed to be strong! They can't see me like this.... I thought to myself. Time passed and the video that Cindy Trim opened with was completed. The lights popped on and all were silent.

The video hit home in so many areas in the women around the circle. I don't know if we were speechless or didn't know where to start because we had so much to say. It was quite powerful. It definitely tapped into our spirits and made us think.

I, having read the book already and done the workbook a year prior due to one of the many sagas in my life, felt like I knew it all…. If so, why was I there? Why was I back in the same position I was in a year before? Why had I not elevated? Why had my life not been a shining example?

Eventually, I raised my hand, after hearing many of the women speak. I said, "You know, I am so frustrated! I feel like a Ferrari sitting in the garage. My frustration comes from knowing I am a Ferrari, designed and built to be one of the most powerful engines out there! It was designed for an intent purpose! It stands out amongst the crowd and its presence is known and expected to do what it was designed to do, except . . . I was still in the garage with the door down, at that."

However, that day is over. It would be one thing if I didn't know who I was, whose I was or the power that lie within me, but I do. I also observe myself year after year sitting in that garage. No more! That day is over! I am in my coming out the garage season. *Vroom . . .Vroom! Watch out!* Here I come! How can I get anywhere sitting in the garage? How can I help anyone else to get there if I am still there? There's so much to see, so much to be done, so many places to go. All I need to do is put my seatbelt on, listen to my God-inspired GPS and start up the car, stopping off for gas (The Word) to fuel up for my next journey. It's time to go out into the world and reach the masses. *The Blame Game Is Over!*

I asked God a typical question, not why but how?

"What you can't see, I can. Trust me and meet me half way. If you get up, I'll make it happen. If you pick up the pencil, I'll hold your hand. If you jog your allotted time, I'll push your legs the extra mile. If you smile, I'll take the photo. If you open your mouth and sing, the glory will come out and the world will be touched by my presence. I cannot bless what you don't test. Try me!"

I have run out of people to blame at this point. I have run out of things to say that got in my way, stopped or hindered me from carrying out the God-given greatness in me. I feel as though I have been turned down by every attempt I've made to seek man's help for my success. I have sought out the greatness in others and have attempted to pull on them for their gifts to aid me in my journey, not realizing each gift had been planted by God. Each gift is an authentic creation of God. Their gift is no higher or better than my own. It is simply different. I came to yet another revelation that the outcome is partially dependent upon the gardner. How often do you personally teal your garden or water your land; your gift? However kind of a gesture, It is not the responsibility of another to come to your house, cut your grass, take out your trash, set the dining table for dinner, nor open your bible for you or pray with you before bed (Yes, I know you can pray at any time…) Yes, folk will help you. Yes, they may even pray for you but…each of us carries the responsibility to ensure proper gardening and nurture of our own.

The difference is, however, the faith, confidence and effort one puts into what God has ordained for their lives. This places them into a whole, entirely separate realm. It is felt and seen in the kingdom. I believe that is what I was drawn to; It was God's light that was drawing me and not that of their own. If I can have such confidence in the gifts God has given others, why can't I do the same for what He has given me? God is God, correct?

He is not a different God in someone else than He would be in you. He does not change, correct? He is the same God then, now, and forever more. Hebrews 13:8
So is it God's ability to empower us in the gifts we possess from Him that we question? Or is it the belief, the faith, the trust, that we lack in the hand of God? We cannot believe He is able partially. He is no respecter of persons. When we stop looking to measure how we perform up against another in any circumstance and begin to focus on how effective our ministry is, we will begin to see things differently. Performance vs. ministry. When you are performing, the benefit, applause and glory comes back to you for how well of a job YOU did. When you minister, you are giving back every ounce of what God gave you to His people in an effort that they may come to see, hear, feel, touch and know Him the better, not YOU!. It is He that

you introduce in ministry and never ourselves. He cannot fail. There is no competition in ministry, for there is one goal to accomplish and several different avenues or means in which to do so. Our primary and sole search in this world is to find the way in which we can best introduce God to mankind.

Looking at it from this perspective should change things a bit for you. You don't have to have the best voice or a voice at all, for that matter. Note that ministry does not take place solely in the four walls of the church house, but in the church that is within you. This could be at work, the grocery store, or even while coaching little league sports. We are examples of Christ at all times. Remember the acronym "WWJD"; the saying, "What would Jesus Do?" In every situation in life, there is a God-like way to handle things. We are to demonstrate that in every way possible throughout this walk of life. What would make a non-believer, or even a believer that is straddling the fence, desire to come into the four walls of the temple if what we represent out the four walls is less than desirable? Meaning, you are wearing a cross that hangs from your neck, but you cut someone off in the parking lot or roll your eyes at the elderly person that is taking a bit of extra time in the grocery line. You are singing all of the material learned at choir rehearsal the night before, but cussing out the person that accidentally bumped into you at the fair causing you to spill a little of the drink God purchased for you anyhow. These are simply things to ponder.

It is the encounter with a true saint on the outside that will make the difference. We gain such a wrap in the when we display behaviors such as these from saints that are performing on Sunday morning and not ministering throughout the week… "True Ministry" is what touches the soul. It reaches way down deep, hitting spots that haven't been nurtured in a long time, if ever before.

It is that warm look in someone's eye that says they are sincere, genuine, and carry the love of God. It is the time taken to stop and allow one to cross the street that may need a little extra time. It is the gentleness felt in a hand up from someone or the warmth in their smile and hug. For me, it is also the note sang ever so gently that confirms everything is going to be all right.

The Holy Spirit is here to guide, comfort, walk with and heal your wounded soul. Therefore, I need not compete in volume or runs, but be mindful that every word and note that proceeds out of my lips has direction from God. Directives as an assignment from God and an intended destination to God's lost and loved ones. This has nothing to do with the next man, except that I work in harmony with him to accomplish the task at hand. Say to yourself, "I Fit! I Belong!" There is nothing to fear if you are delivering what is from God. It has already been "prepped, primed and purposed" to prepare the hearts of man for the King. It won't sound or look like anyone else's offering.

It is uniquely designed like that of a fingerprint in which it can only identify you and what you bring to the table. How awesome is that?

So now, what do you fear? If anything, it should be yourself. So take self out of the equation. Move self out of the way so you can serve God and His people with the utmost confidence. Release yourself once and for all from the bondage that seeks to strangle your blessing and choke out your promise. The devil is a lie and we seek to expose Him, now!

So, there is no longer, nor was there, anyone to blame but yourself. We, at times, can be our biggest enemy. It is time to stand up, receive, accept and develop that which has been given to us by God. We have been given everything that we need to get the job done. We don't need someone else (whom we feel holds a higher position) to do it for us to sit and hold our hands. The truth is, if they are truly doing God's work, they may be busy doing just that; helping to save the lost and needy. You are big enough and strong enough, equipped and ready now for battle. Continue training by reading your sword (the Word of God) and sitting under your Pastor, Bishop, Minister, Priest or spiritual leader Take all that you have learned coupled with your God-given gifts and apply to your daily living and to all that you will come in contact with. The blame game is over! The battle has now begun! Here's a *Secret* – It is your gift that will ultimately heal you. Your gift…Not that of another. *Stop blaming others for the lack of use of your own gift.* The blame game is over!

Truly it is about taking the *"you"* out and magnifying the *"Him"* in you that propels the gifts forward.

As a writer, it is easy to think that your days are unproductive especially when the world teaches that production is dependent upon a time cards clock in and clock out.

The day must come when we realize that our clock in started the day we were born, and our clock out won't take place until the day we depart this earth. In between, there is *much* work to be done. Our daily clock in and out begins when our eyes open and when they close for slumber. In those hours that you slumber, allow God to speak to you in your dreams. It is what we do with those dreams in our awake hours that counts as production.

Know that this will change from day to day. Unlike the routine clock in and out of man's world, Kingdom is not routine in this way. Man clocks in mundanely, completing tasks given to them that once done can be signed off on and on to the next. When the 8th hour is completed, you are believed to have successfully been productive in that day. Kingdom production however, is ongoing. It is not, nor can it be, determined in a day. There is a strong possibility, like the buildings of the Ancient Greek, that we may not be around to see the totality of the end results and effects of our productive labor. This won't mean that it didn't take place. It simply means that the work is much greater than you and I. It is timeless. Never feel that you are not productive because you have no physical time card to punch. There will be people touched, healed, saved, and delivered because of the poem you wrote today, the song you ministered, the written story or verbal testimony you delivered, a message you preached. A soul saved and won for Jesus is the ultimate count of productiveness one could ever acquire.

No one will remember how many burgers you flipped in a day, or how many copies you made, how many cups of coffee you poured or how many boxes you stacked, but the Word of God will live on forever. It is my prayer that this book and my songs, will touch the lives of many long after I am gone and so will the works of your hand through a transformed and healed soul. This I often pray in Jesus name.

CHAPTER EIGHTEEN

Game Day

There are many good things to live for in this life. Now, with these days of hurt, how can we maintain, fight and move forward without being loose cannons and causing mass destruction to an already dying world? It is your job as an Ambassador to pull yourself up by the bootstraps, arm yourself and fight. Your fight must again come with strategic warfare plans of action. Why must I have to pull myself up? Why strategic? Why plan? Can't we just fight? "I just want to do the work, turn it in and be done with it!" (Quoted by one of my former students) Well, that all sounds nice, but it is impossible to have a successful battle without first strengthening and taking care of yourself, assessing the situation and making a plan to follow. You must then equip yourself!

Finally, my brethren, be strong in the Lord and in the power of His might. Put on the whole armor of God, that you may be able to stand against the wiles of the devil. For we do not wrestle against flesh and blood, but against principalities, against powers, against the rulers of the darkness of this age, [a] against spiritual hosts of wickedness in the heavenly places. Therefore, take up the whole armor of God, that you may be able to withstand in the evil day, and having done all, to stand.

Stand therefore, having girded your waist with truth, having put on the breastplate of righteousness, and having shod your feet with the preparation of the gospel of peace; above all, taking the shield of faith with which you will be able to quench all the fiery darts of the wicked one. And take the helmet of salvation, and the sword of the Spirit, which is the word of God; praying always with all prayer and supplication in the Spirit, being watchful to this end with all perseverance and supplication for all the saints. (Ephesian 6:10-18)

This includes the study of your Word that you may know who you are, whose you are and the powers that come with that position. There's nothing like going into battle to fight with your fist not knowing you were carrying a sword. You must also know what you're battling, as well as their strengths and weaknesses and even their secret attack potential.

As a former collegiate basketball player and coach of an NCAA Division 1 Team, this concept is to this day deeply engrained in my very being and rooted in my soul. This is why as a newborn Believer, I was able to grasp the concept so quickly and take it to heart. My life and training embodies every bit of this tactic. Follow me, if you will, as I use my sport and experience in it thereof to break down our plan of hope!

The last game they hurt us! They hurt us bad. They crushed us on all sides and embarrassed us in front of our own. You insert here… (Families, friends, God, other believers, non-believers and others). In other words, they made us look like fools. We were thrown to the wolves for feeding and exposed. Yes, I said naked we came and naked we go, but I didn't mean to be left uncovered.

This is what happens to us saints when we are not covered, not equipped, not prepared, *not ready*! We have to live as though it is always game day. That means we must daily strengthen ourselves, our mind, our body and soul. If that means getting into the weight room or on the treadmill, even jogging your own block, ok no time? Walk to work if you're close, use the stairs instead of the elevator, and so on. There was nothing worse than being on a police force, working your butt off to get on and then being teamed up with an out-of-shape partner that couldn't stay in the battle with you if they tried. This was not my case, but you get the analogy.

We must do this, not to just get in but to stay in! Our bodies need to be strengthened to compete, to fight, to battle, to win! 40 minutes, *Go Hard*! That was my motto. As a starting player, there would be many a game that I would not be able to come out of. My team depended on me to be able to weather the storm for the entire 40 minutes and come out on top.

We may have gotten time outs called and water breaks here and there, and then it was back on. If I do need to tag team and come out, it is kingdom minded that you be able to replace me, nothing lacking, nothing missing, nothing . . . A strong choir even knows that for an extended note, we can't all drop out at the same time. Each must take a breath as others cover for them until they can get back in. The note then goes forward until the enemy is slain and the job completed. This is how we would approach the opponent, this is how we would reach victory and overcome the game of defeat! That was the goal for our physical strength. Now for our mental toughness! We must equip our minds, as well. You have to know the field you are operating in or on. There are rules to everything. In most cases, however, there will be a coach to guide you through if you care to listen, along with a book or manual of instruction.

Do you know the rules to the commandments to the kingdom of God and all who claim to be His children? Do you know your parameters, your guidelines, your way out should you need one, where to go for instruction, or how to recover from a temporary defeated position? That's what I love about the game of basketball, in your allotted time, you have unlimited chances to score, to recover, to get the ball back, redeem yourself and get it right. This, in turn, would uplift and encourage a teammate to achieve small victories along the way.

There are always glimpses of *hopeful* situations as long as you stay in the game and on your post. On your post? Yes, on your post! You've heard this before only they may have said in your lane. Do the job that God designed for you to do and do it with all of your heart. Allow other teammates to fulfill the roles they were designed to do, as well. It is called teamwork. You back and cover them in prayer and they will back and cover you. A loose ball will innately draw the kingdom to jump into action, but while making sure the ball remains in our possession, do not leave other areas exposed. Make sure all portals of entrance are closed off to the enemy. Not only do we need to know the game's ins and outs, how many time outs we're given, what the score is and how much time is left on the clock, but do you realize that we also need to know everything there is to know about the opponent, too?

We need to know them as well as we know ourselves. We need to know what it is they are after, so we then may know how to protect it. We need to know what their strategies of attack are so that we know how to counteract it. We need to know what their strengths are so we know exactly how to prepare for them. We need to know what their weaknesses are so that we can know what angle or approach to take as we begin to deactivate their intended purpose. I spent as much time in film session learning my opponent as I did on the court. Although I have to be honest, several days I was kicked out due to my immaturity at the time. My best friend, teammate, roommate, and all around partner in crime, Penny Armstrong, would see to it to somehow have the best jokes on that day. One of those friends you just could not be around without busting out in laughter. She didn't have to say a word and you'd burst into tears . . . Boy do I miss those days. Boy do I miss her. If you're reading this P., Hi!

Eventually, we got ourselves together. Pure talent helped us out for the most part, as it will you in ministry, but imagine how much further along we could all have been or be if we had formed that spiritual maturity a bit earlier and actually lived by it.

Well, my motto today which is on my Independent basketball training cards, reads," *It's Never Too Late to Learn"*. As I stated, we spent a large amount of time in scouting reports with no ball in hand whatsoever. We read about our opponent and broke them down from their playing abilities to the tattoos on their body.

We left nothing unturned. We had a plan for their every action. In fact, we had a plan that would not allow their plan to ever take effect. Speaking of no ball in hand, we did this in live practices, too. We would run around and envision the game with no ball in hand so that the thrill of scoring could not override the ultimate team plan we had worked so very hard to accomplish. That would be equivalent to what we know in the world as flesh. We took the "I" out of it and returned the power over to the head, who had the best interest of the overall team, vision and goal. The one who could lead us, guide us, and direct us to victory in our daily lives. Coach God!

Did you know there are people strategically placed in your life to bring you down, to see to it that you do not meet your goals, to plant improper seeds in your life and to fertilize your growth with toxins? Today, we give them no more access to our lives, to our goals, our dreams, our vision. We cancel out the assignment that they may have had by strategically placing ourselves as well. We need to sit high enough to see them coming, close enough to hear their plan but far enough not to be entangled in their iniquity. (Galatians 5:1)

This is where our hope is formed in that we have the ability to make change. We can change the outcome of a defeated game. Shame and blame are no more.

We are now able to invite the world to the *Big Day*, as we know we have prepared in every way possible. We know the end from the beginning because of His Word. We win! We now have something to offer those that we invite to the "Big Game" and we are not selling wolf tickets. In fact the offer on the table is something we could never pay for anyhow. It's called a gift. It is a gift to the world; a gift to all who believe and will receive it. Yes, the metaphor is to basketball because that, too, has my heart here on earth. We all have passions, and that is one of mine. However, in the kingdom, God's love is *free*. His Son died for us that we might have life and have it more abundantly. He died that we may come to know God without the cost of losing. John 10:10

There is *no* losing in God. *All victory* on this side! Now this is a team I love being on and don't mind playing full time! No riding the bench on this one! I'm all in! Here is where you can rest. It may not be a physical rest all of the time, but it surely is a spiritual one, knowing that as long as you are on this team, your battle is already won, your daily needs met and your future bright.

Your healing process will begin as the wounds that were once open will begin to clot, sealed by the blood of Jesus. You will not ache and ail longing for life, as you now have knowledge of your everlasting life. You need not rely on your own strength and might, as you will lean on the strength of the Lord and His might will go ahead of your battles. Isaiah 40:29 Your daily struggles will be there. The difference is your ability to navigate through them, head held high, chest out, knowing that grace and mercy follows you and favor reigns in your life.

When hurt enters the soul of your body, there is always a process that leads to becoming whole again. The journey leads to regaining not only your original state, but an even stronger one. In a career of high school, collegiate and semi pro ball, I have experienced my share of injuries; hurts. One of my largest, aside from a broken jaw, was an (ACL) Anterior Cruciate Ligament tear. I had torn it in both knees! That *hurt*, like all get out! It was devastating and the road to recovery long and tedious. The process was, however, one that promised a vital outcome if carried out, followed through and endured to the end. It is not an easy one nor does it always feel good. However, when I signed that letter of intent for my scholarship to school, I knew if I showed up every day with an open mind and gave all that I had to give, through all of my ups and downs, I would be taken care of for the duration of my collegiate career and then some. My college diploma was as good as in my hands before I even began.

I am still being taken care of due to my collegiate basketball experience and endeavors. This is like the promise of God. When you sign on, you instantaneously have *hope*. Upon receiving His promises, you are guaranteed to be taken care of for a lifetime and then some. *Healing,* is inevitable as long as you keep living. Each step that you take immediately walks you into your healing, into your destiny. Be ye healed on this day! Congratulations! You are being offered an honorary letter of intent! Sign on today!

Despite your background and current situation, you can conquer your past. You can achieve your goals and dreams. You can complete any task you put your hands to, if you let the hand of the Lord be your guide. You can be all that God has purposed for you to be. Your life experience has prepared you for this very moment!

Do I have any regrets? I can truly say only that I have not shared everything with you. I am sure in fact, the most intimate, the most shocking, the most heart wrenching things are are amongst the deleted material. I have traveled this country for love. I have disrespected myself on a many of occasion, hiding in hotels etc., pretending my presence didn't exist or wasn't worthy of being publicly known. Some things are left for God to disclose in His perfect way; in His perfect timing. Who knows…Maybe we will meet one day, have coffee, swap stories, cry, laugh, hug and pray together. You can help me and I can help you by the testimonies in our bellies. I truly await that day.

1 Thessalonians 5:11 Wherefore comfort yourselves together, and edify one another, even as also ye do.

Psalm 22:22 I will praise you to all of my brothers; I will stand up before the congregation and testify of the wonderful things you have done.

Remember my beloved ones; No matter how attractive the flesh may appear, how lonely your heart may be, how high of a calling a man or woman of God has…NO ONE can love you the way the Master can.

In closing, I am reminded of a quote from my friend Mr. David Burrus,

"There are no meaningless moments."

TODAY I LOOKED IN THE MIRROR

Today I looked in the mirror
A figure looked back at me
Face of a woman in a shadow
Face of adversity

Around her neck hung a cross
Around her neck hung the cost
Weighted down yet lifted up
A crown was worn that bore her cup

Behind her smile behind her eyes

Game Day!

I discerned her spirit, I heard her cries
Behind her structure
Her truth lies

Once smooth, now weathered
A storm she's tethered
Intense is her stare
Wooley is her hair
What she's been through?
Just don't seem quite fair

Her nose is rounded
Her nose is flared
Her souls been tested
Her flesh been dared

Anxiety stricken and now exposed
The mirror doesn't lie
It shows in her pose

Now the mirror looks back at me
Not defeated, not cheated
It's me I see....
You can handle this
You were designed to flee
The web of the one who's entangled thee

Beautiful, beautiful that's what I see
Creation of God, yielding to thee
Longing and yearning to be set free
A reflection of light cancelled misery
That reflection in the mirror is a reflection of me!

Today I looked in the mirror
And looking back at me
Stood the years of am unclean frame
Cleansed into purity~

Questions & Reflections

What are your accomplishments? List them. It is important to remind yourself of your resume from time to time.

_____

_____

_____

_____

_____

_____

_____

_____

_____

What did it take to accomplish these things?

_____

_____

_____

_____

_____

What are dreams or visions you still have?

_____

_____

_____

_____

_____

_____

_____

_____

_____

What are the necessary steps it will take for you to get there?

_____

_____

_____

_____

_____

_____

_____

Are these things you want, or are they things others want for you?

_____

_____

_____

_____

_____

_____

_____

Do you believe you can achieve them?

_____

_____

_____

_____

_____

Are you willing to put in the time, effort and finance to support them? _____ Yes ـــــ No

What are your current roadblocks?

_____

_____

_____

_____

_____

What have been your stumbling blocks in the past?

_____

_____

_____

_____

_____

_____

_____

_____

_____

Now let's dissect, disconnect and redirect! You are in the perfect place for your new beginning. Your past experiences have set you up perfectly for what is to come next. Ready? Set? Let's go!

First, answer this question. Who Are You? What is your purpose?

_____

_____

_____

_____

_____

_____

_____

_____

_____

_____

_____

_____

_____

_____

_____

Now, get something on your mind that you know good and well you are to be doing but haven't. Pray about that something you are doing that you know is not what God intended for you to be doing. Pray about that thing you know without a shadow of a doubt He's assigned unto you. Pray for what you honestly have not trusted Him enough to release and do! Sometimes you have to just stop and commune with the good Lord right where you are.

Like anything else, we must re-program the way we think, whether we desire to begin dieting, improving study habits, changing negative behaviors,   sleep habits, drinking, smoking, cussing, mistreating one another and/or sexually impure dealings. It comes down to choice. Like any other choice you'd make, you'd first weigh out the costs, the benefits and the savings.

List any situational issues that you may be facing at this time:
 What has it cost you?
Financially? Emotionally? Physically? Spiritually?

_____

_____

_____

_____

_____

_____

_____

_____

What does it benefit you?

_____

_____

_____

_____

How has it affected your time?

_____

_____

_____

_____

Your family/relationships?

_____

_____

_____

_____

Your sleep/rest?

_____

_____

_____

_____

_____

Mental wear and tear (fear, anxiety)?

_____

_____

_____

_____

Your goal timeline?

_____

_____

_____

_____

Your dreams?

_____

_____

_____

_____

Your overall well-being?

_____

_____

_____

_____

Your ability to operate and function productively and
consistently?

_____

_____

_____

_____

Your mood and outlook pertaining to your "Jesus effect" on others? Do others see, feel or hear God through you?

_____

_____

_____

_____

Knowing the goal, that the people you come across will feel, hear, see, and receive a touch from the Master just because of you, do you think you have gained in any of these areas or have you experienced loss because of it? Explain...

_____

_____

_____

_____

_____

_____

Are you a lifter of spirits or have you noticed others to be drained agitated and or irritable after a dealing with you?

_____

_____

_____

_____

_____

_____

_____

_____

_____

_____

_____

_____

_____

_____

It is definitely something to ponder. Do you leave a positive impact on the lives of others or are things getting in the way of you being truly vested in the greater call you have pertaining to the lives of others? Reflect on just what may be in the way?

_____

_____

_____

_____

_____

_____

_____

_____

We do our brother's keepers and we have a responsibility to share the God in us with others that they, too, may know God and His mighty works.

Let's dig deeper

What, or who, has hurt you?

_____

_____

_____

_____

_____

_____

_____

_____

_____

_____

Ask yourself as you write below, "What is it in each of these things or people that has hurt me so deeply?" Was it even the person that hurt us? Was it the circumstance? Maybe it was the prestige that would've come with the position we thought we could have had. Or could it be the feeling of fear of failure, insignificance or defeat? Was it an outward hurt? Were you upset, angry or irritated with someone or something else that wasn't in your control? Was your hurt inward? Are there things within yourself that you are not satisfied with and haven't the slightest idea of how to change?

_____

_____

_____

_____

_____

_____

This helps to break down the hurt that we may be able to properly decipher its origin and then begin to slowly channel its energy in proper directions. Un~ channeled energy leads to what my mom always refers to as loose cannons. They are cannons that have no particular aim but are guaranteed to go off, and when they do, look out! They will fire in every direction possible. Loose cannons are very dangerous. Left unresolved, they can affect everyone around us and leave us much worse off than when we started. Instead of aiming at a specified target, it is possible that whoever is closest may just get hit.

When this happens, it can be quite devastating, as you never intended to hurt anyone. You were only trying to throw the hurt off of you and in the process of battling, you never stopped to strategically look at the whole picture that you may come up with a designed attack or approach. You just shot and killed in angry fire. Now you are responsible for the aftermath and effects of several wounded souls. You see, it's a domino effect. Not only will the ones you've hurt be wounded, but they, too, may go out and wound others, creating a perpetual cycle of pain and suffering.

"We are destined to repeat what we don't defeat." Bishop Michael Pitts.

We must remember in moving forward to forgive others as we forgive ourselves. God has forgiven us all. He has paid the highest price and died that we may live. Now that is Love. God is love. In learning to love ourselves, we are able to love one another. What better gift can you give to Christ?

List things God placed inside of you that you are ready to use to serve the kingdom, such as projects, and assignments:

_____

_____

_____

_____

_____

_____

Now, share your steps in ensuring this will happen, for example, people you may want to meet with business plans to write. Indicate your goals below, and give yourself a timeline:

_____

_____

_____

_____

_____

_____

List things you will cut back on, sacrifice and/or give up all together in order to strengthen your walk:

_____

_____

_____

_____

_____

_____

List three Bible verses you will commit to memory that will help you in, with and/or through your endeavors. Write them out and read them daily:

_____

_____

_____

About the Author

Born in Oakland, California, raised between California and Illinois, Jasmine is a lover of the Lord. This woman of God touches the hearts of humanity by lending herself back to God's hands to do His mighty works here on earth day in and day out. Teaching the meaning of "TRUE LOVE" is her mission as she gracefully walks the world in purpose, guided by the hand of the Master.

She is a single mother of two; Graduate of University of Illinois; Author of the book "Uncommon Grace", Recording Artist and Songwriter. Her new single "Praisn' All by Myself" was recently released from her upcoming EP, Spirit. She is an Educator of over 20 years and has received Teacher of the Year awards at two of her teaching location sights. She was also the Vice President of her police academy class. In her former position as a police officer, she received a leadership award awarded to her by the Mayor in the town in which she served. Amongst all else, Jasmine has an athletic side to her. She formerly played Women's Basketball for the University of Illinois - Chicago and was the Captain of her squad before becoming the youngest Head Coach in the Midwest collegiate conference. She was Interim Head Coach of the NCAA

Women's Basketball team at Loyola University. Jasmine has now taken the direction of public speaking and life coaching. She aspires to inspire the world by not only modeling in photos but by modeling the walk of Christ.

Jasmine is currently under the leadership of Bishop Christopher C. Smith, New Birth Church, Pittsburg, California, where she sings on the Praise Team with True Worship under the phenomenal direction of Elder Tim and Minister Dasha Moore. Jasmine has an extensive background of phenomenal leaders. Smokey Norful, Michael V. McKay, James Hamilton, Ron Rosson, Judah, Ernest Dayce, Dr. Gregory Sephus and more. She was the vocal director and Praise and Worship leader at Seed of Faith serving under her pastor Dr. Ralph E. Howard and directed the youth choir, as well, during her stint with the ministry. She has both put on herself and spoken in various music workshops. Her charismatic personality and vocal gifting landed her positions, such as Vocal Director for several plays, the latest being *The WIZ* directed by Clay Davidson at CCC Theatre. Jasmine recently landed a role and vocal spot in the world premiere of *Xtigone/African-American Shakespeare Theatre Company* written by Nambi E. Kelly directed by Rhodessa Jones and accompanied by the musical direction of Tommy James Shephered   Jr.

Acknowledgements

MOM and DAD: Mom and Dad, *Thank You*. You are by far the most incredible people I know. I'm not kidding and I don't say that because you are my parents. You two are the epitome of accomplished individuals. I couldn't have asked for better examples in my life. Mom I watched you closely on a daily basis push through this world with your head held high, conquering any feat that stood in your way. There was nothing you couldn't do as a woman and mother. You have shown me that I can make it as a single mother and, moreover, with God that I can make it period. No matter what, you always made a way. No matter what was going on, I felt as if you always had it under control. Dad you worked hard...endlessly long hours to put bread on the table and shelter over our heads. A family man you are! I look for qualities of you in the gentlemen I meet. You make it hard...haven't found anyone like you yet. Thank you for hanging in there during those rough teenage years, taking me shopping for womanly products and all. Thank you for our talks, yes, even the birds and the bees... I am still blushing. I love you both, as it has taken the combination of the two to make who I am to this day and I like me! Thank you for never letting me fall hard enough to cause harm but just enough to bump my head and wake up! Thank you for helping me to stay afloat even to this day. You allowed me to gracefully keep my dignity, though it has been you two so many times that have come to the rescue financially and emotionally in times when I thought I just might lose it all. I never did, thanks to you both. I will forever strive to give back to the world what you have instilled in me, a bit day by day, piece by piece. It will be tough, but I think I can do it! Oh! You are *Great* grandparents, too! I'll just say the apple doesn't fall far!

Grandparents: Thanks to my Grandmother and Grandfather Clyde and Hattye Stingily. Grandmother and Grandfather Jesse Lacey and Alonzo Strange; I have fond memories of roots that transfer back to Alabama and Mississippi, places I was fortunate enough to travel to and from for years with my grandparents. A legacy I was left to carry on. Grandma and Grandpa Stingily and Grandpa Strange may you rest in peace. I love you always. Grandma Great, as my children call you, you are one special lady to me. If you feed me one more plate of food, I think I will pop! Our times together, I hold very dear to my heart…no need to go into detail: you and I know. I love you, Grandma. You have been my backbone, a voice of wisdom, an example of love. You have been a prayer warrior for me battling off the enemy left and right and calling on the angels that guide me day and night. I will do my best to follow in your footsteps. I pray you are proud of me.

My children, Lyric and Cadence: I could write an entire book on the thanks I have toward these two descendants of mine. They have been there with mommy through it all, well at least since their existence. They have held me up in the lowest of times and laughed with me through the good ones. They are true young pillars of our family. I am so proud of the both of them. They are individually so incredibly gifted, talented, smart and wise beyond their years. They have found such an inner peace about themselves and, through it all, still find the willpower to push toward greatness. I know God is with them because when I was weak, they were strong. They both have the ability to see past themselves and into the needs of others. They know how to make me smile and how to get that last nerve, too! That's okay because it is theirs to get anyhow. Beautiful Lyric, the words to my song, and Handsome Cadence, the rhythm and beat of my heart, mommy loves you, never forget that. The world is yours to behold. As my daddy once told me, whatever you become, make sure you are the best at it! When times get low, *call on God*! He is your protector, your provider, your way maker, your redeemer, your savior, your all in all. I thank you for standing by me in the low times and I look forward to spending the many high times that are coming with *you*!

Gamma Devo (De Voice Bradford): Thank you for stepping in and loving us like your own. Your love cannot be duplicated.

You are a priceless addition to our lives. You have a heart of gold. I believe nothing happens by happenstance but rather divine intervention. You, woman of God, are a God send. We love and cherish you like family. I can only pray that we are able to reciprocate your love. Thank you for your obedience to God in taking us in as yours. We don't plan on going anywhere, so don't you make plans to either. We're in it for the long haul. We love you!

Bishop Christopher C. Smith: I thank the Lord for my Bishop Smith! Though I was born with the gifts God has bestowed upon me, it wasn't until I joined New Birth Church that I was awakened. My gift in and of writing was released. Sitting under the covering of Bishop, healing while eating the rich food he served, is almost indescribable. I never left church the same. Week after week, I felt like a super hero being transformed. Awakened to my call, other than singing, awakened to myself, awakened to the power I actually possessed in God, I took off! I began to write *this Book*. Bishop said, "Give me *one* year and your life will never be the same." It hasn't. I am forever grateful. Thank you Bishop and First Lady Adrienne Smith for the continued covering and positive example that you provide in my life.

Pastor Alfred Smith, Sr. and Jr.: Even as a child, I knew what it was to reverence something. The word may have been too big for me but it was in this house, Allen Temple Baptist Church, that I was first baptized. I knew there was something sacred going on here. I was reared up, trained and disciplined in this house. It is the foundation of my Christian experience. What better place to receive this introduction: Choir rehearsal, Sunday School, prayer, scripture memorizations, community outings, even *"The Welcome"*, all those things you do in church…I learned here. As you read the book, you will see, these, too, are the years I would stray trying to find myself as I reached my teen years. However, my foundation was rock solid! Thus, the scripture, Proverbs 22:6, *"Train up a child in the way he should go: and when he is old, he will not depart from it."* Thanks to you Pastor Alfred Smith, Sr., and Pastor Smith, Jr., I have not departed!

Pastor Marvin E. Wiley: (Rock of Ages Baptist Church) To my first pastor in my young adult life, you may never know the impact that you have had on my life. You laid down your life so that others may live…. I recall following you like a puppy. Where you went, I went. It was a very tender time in my life. Thousands of miles away from home, unwed, new baby, out of college with the world in front of me and little to no guidance and direction, you provided sound doctrine and a safe place for me to grow spiritually. It is said that first impressions are everything. You carried the baton well! 18 years ago you introduced God all over to me. This time as a young adult, even in the absence of my parents, you insured that I knew the importance of Jesus in my life. I saw church as my family. In fact, I loved my church so much that it tore me apart moving back to California. To have a church have that much impact on your life says something. Little did I know, I'd have a single out inspired by you, *"Live Again"*, let alone a book that you would find worthy enough to forward. Thank you Man of God.

Bishop Ralph Howard: (Seed of Faith Christian Fellowship) Pastor, I want to thank you for the spiritual leadership you have provided me since I stepped foot back in California. You nurtured my gifting and made room and time for me and my children. No matter how many you were Shepherd to, you made yourself assessable to my family, coming to hospitals, plays, birthdays, christening my home, even attending my basketball games, praying over all of the teams, baptizing both of my children and always donating to their life adventures and personally mediating between the flock. You identified the ministerial calling in me and even wrote recommendations for my Theological schooling. You appointed me to lead Praise and Worship when I refused to talk to people and somehow saw me fit to even direct the choir, lead the youth and teach Sunday

School! You are quite a special Pastor. Family is important. You made us feel as though we were family. We will always be family.

Prophet Hardin: I will never forget the day you came into town and in the midst of the very first Judah Fest, you released a word to me under a heavily anointed atmosphere. It had to be my first out of body experience, as you took off your coat and placed it on me. You professed an identity in Christ that I had and spoke prophesy that not only would I be leading Praise and Worship, which I wasn't at that time, but that there were books in my belly and a cd would manifest. You said that I was behind 10 years but would have those years restored to me. At the time, man of God, I couldn't see any of that. Me? Lead Praise and Worship? Me? Write a book? Produce a cd? And now… Thank you so much for your obedience in God in allowing Him to speak through you that others may receive even if but a glimpse into who they are. May the prophesy live on as I accept the call. God bless you.

Pastor Ron Rosson: I remember your arrival to my church. It was a breath of fresh air, to say the least. I had come under the leadership and direction of Smokey Norful just prior and struggled with the idea that I wouldn't be able to find leadership of that magnitude again. I did! It was you! You picked me out and identified gifting in me. You took me under your wing and provided tough love~ The love that hurts at times but grows you up real fast. You believed in me and that was what mattered most. You were different. You taught me what it was to not only have vision or follow vision but to create vision as you were continually creating with your uncanny prophetic flow. "See it before you see it", he'd always say. I'll never forget sitting with you and listening to you, witnessing you create the vision of what is now known as Judah Fest. My eyes grew large and I trembled inside as you spoke it right into existence. I thank God for allowing me to witness, bear witness, showing me that I could do the same in His name. I am on my way… You once drew an imaginary line on the floor and said, "I don't know what you're waiting on. Your greatness is just on the other side. JUMP!" I am finally taking the leap! Your friendship speaks for itself…Thank you.

Coach Bruce Campbell: To the man who transformed me from cheerleader to basketball player. To you, my high school counselor and basketball coach. To the man who said, "Kiddo, you're going to make it! You are going to earn a basketball scholarship and you are going to go to college." It was no question in your mind. Thank you for taking me under your wing. Thank you for allowing me in your office to cry when I was stressed. Thank you for developing me into a leader for seeing what I didn't see. Thank you for the rides daily home from practice. Thank you for your consistent presence in my teenage life. I can't tell you how important that was to me. Thank you for seeing me through my ACL knee surgeries and assuring me that everything was going to be alright. Most of all, thank you for sharing a bit of your life with me. Look how far I've come, Coach!

Coach Eileen Copenhaver: Being thousands of miles away from home at one of the most vulnerable times in one's life is *not* easy. I want to thank you for the discipline and instruction you provided me in those years. You never let me quit although there were many days I wanted to. I recall a day when I told you I was done and not coming back, in which you replied, "I will see you here at practice in 6 minutes!" I never ran so hard in my life! It might not have been 6 minutes but I know I made it from those dorms to that practice facility in no more than 10 minutes, that's for sure. We weren't an easy bunch…well, I know I wasn't. Thank you for not only picking me during recruiting season along with your assistants but for pushing me the entire way through! I am who I am today because of it and that's the bottom line truth!

Smokey Norful: When you get a start in music like the one I received, let me tell you, you are blessed. To be directed every Thursday and Sunday of my life by a man of God of your magnitude in a ministry that is so dear to my heart is rare. This I know. There are many great worshippers out there but man of God, we were blessed with one of the best! You set the bar high early on in my life. For that, I am forever grateful. I am careful now to follow dress protocol after you told me I was going to get you in trouble coming up in that choir stand with pants on. I still laugh about that to this day. What a great experience you provided to us...to me. Then to see the manifestation of your works as you journeyed on... My God! I have no words...yes me, for once with no words. All I can say is thank you: for your time, your teaching, your patience, your example and for sharing your gift with me.

Peter L. Callendar: As my creative director in yet another gifting of mine, *acting*! I want to thank you for encouraging me to live from the inside out. You taught me what it is to give and to give selflessly. You allowed me to let down my guard, channel my past, instead of covering, it up and use it to pull from. Whether I am acting, ministering in song, or writing, it is crucial to give all of me. That was difficult for me, as I had become accustomed to holding back as a protective mechanism to my heart and soul. I learned from you that it is the sharing of one's heart and soul that breathes life into the things that we do! You showed me the true gift of sharing myself with the world. I have

274

found healing in that and have been able to help others because of it. Thank you for believing in me and casting me.

Minister Dasha and Elder Tim Moore: To my power couple leaders. My current Ministers of Music. I am honored to serve under such dynamic leadership. You both lead in not only excellence but love. I remember the first Sunday morning you handed me the mic out of the blue, that is, and said sing Sister Jaz... My eyes bugged out, face flushed and heart began to pound. Not that I don't come from a singing background but as I've said before, I don't take your ministerial leadership lightly. You and Elder Tim believed in me. Something at the time I needed very dearly. I, as well, am grateful for the day you called me to the back of our music room in the church. I thought I was in trouble. Instead you took the time out to talk to me as I was so desperately seeking a mentor. You shared with me what has made you. It blessed me to watch closely the women of God that have been placed in my life as it pertains to healthy living, marriages, rearing children and even the music ministry. Thank you for taking time out for me!

Dr. Lakita Long: Thank you Dr. Long for being a true sister. Thank you for praying, warring and interceding on my behalf. Thank you for our table talks surrounding proud powerful mothers, kingdom business and the inkling that there's more!

Thank you for not just believing but knowing the more existed inside of me.

Pastor Karlton Ray:

When man is in tune with the spirit, he not only shines but his light is so bright, it shines upon others. Thank you for allowing your light to shine upon me. You saw the God in me and said *"It is time."* Your open door I do not take lightly. In fact, I honor, treasure and will forever cherish your gracious act of obedience to the Holy Spirit as you operate in blind faith on my behalf. May your family and ministry be forever blessed.

Most of all, thank you to the God of all creation, my Lord and Saviour, Jesus Christ, my light, my healer, my redeemer, the one who gave me life and saved my soul and has covered my life with an UNCOMMON GRACE!

Pastor Penny and Jerry Slaven

Thank you for pulling me to the forefront, spotting and acknowledging the call of God on my life. I look forward to our future ministerial endeavors.

Pastor Felix Golden

To a man after God's own heart. Thank you for opening your doors to a vision that can only be seen through God. Your heart for ministry and your compassion for mankind truly mirrors what God's love is all about. I will take your example to move further into my purpose and to be a blessing to the Kingdom of God.

Pastor George Miller (Nova)

Man of God may I simply say thank you. I thank God for yielding a platform to thank you openly and publicly. Man after God's own heart this is for your seen and unseen deeds and acts of kindness. You have labored and sewed asking NOTHING in return. You too were there at my lowest. I will never forget...Like an angel you appeared. Even in my shelter experience you made sure I had a way to and from work. I have no idea how you did it but somehow you got that ol' bucket of mine up and running and delivered back to me. I am in tears writing and remembering. Because of your act of agape love, I never missed work nor skipped a beat. God cover and keep you and your family with an uncommon grace.

Pastor Joseph B. Washington

Some people you only meet once and your life is touched forever. Thank you to this man of God for staring me in the face and saying woman of God "YOU ARE NOT AVERAGE" "LET GO OF AVERAGE" ,which happens to be the title of one of his books. I am drawn to those bold enough to dedicate their life to not only following Christ but using it to change the lives of others as well. Incredible to me are those that think not only of their knowledge and welfare, but leap out in faith on the uncharted waters to grab the hand of another. Thank you for sharing that although there is such a thing called time in which no man knows the hour…there is no age limitation on showing the world a piece of God's love by not shrinking down but standing tall and being an example of what it is to overcome the average mindset. We are of God, from God standing for God and by NO means are we Average!

Ernest Dayce~

Thank you for guidance that can only come from one who is diligent in their craft/gift and walks closely with God. You instilled in me a desire to work toward greatness, to look higher, think higher and operate on a higher level. Sometimes it only takes a push from an encouraging voice. That voice was yours...

Prophetess Rein Johnson and
Prophetess Renee' Winston~

When powerful women speak into the lives of other women...they are to be applauded. You two slay demons like eatin' candy! Then smile and laugh at the devil. You are two of the most powerful women I know face to face and I tell you I have been bless and my life impacted forever because of the breath you breathed back into me! You didn't have to do it. You could have left me behind in a dying state but you didn't! Thank you for taking me with you to do the work of our father. I remember a service in which we were both on program and after the word you spoke I was out for the count! (Reign Johnson) I thought I was there to minister when clearly I was there to be ministered to! Thank you Jesus for sisterhood that won't let you fall. I love you both dearly!

Prophet Terrell Turner:
Thank you for speaking life! The boldness to stand before Gods' people and tell it like it is~ not how we want it to be. Thank you for sacrificing your life to save ours. When you lay hands, it is important that the seed be acknowledged. You did just that. You blessed not only myself but called out my children~my fruit and layed them out as well. You spoke things in and over them that no doubt have had an impact on who they have become today.

Iyanla Vanzant

I thank you for the example that you are and for the living example you have been to me for years. As you will find in this book, I have been all over the place and yet feel at times I've been nowhere. I held on through many things one of them being the ability to read yet another story other than my own that I could relate to. Your ability to tell the story and make it plain as my first pastor J. Alfred Smith used to say, allowed me to trust the process. Thank you for your truth, for your love, for your willingness to share that another of us might do the same. Your books, my favorite being, "One Day My Soul Just Opened Up", "In the Meantime", and The Value in the Valley", I have treasured. They have been timeless pieces of literature that have provided me with, guidance, wisdom, hope, courage and strength as I to continue to grow. I've had my moments of struggle and I'm sure as this life goes on I will have more but thank God for women like you whose words have given me tools to navigate through what could likely take us out if another had not shared. Again, I say thank you as you continue to use your life visibly to help the world one person at a time.

I was once told you do not necessarily need to know your mentor personally yet they are people in your life in which you line up and connect regarding your walk, where exactly it is you desire to go and the roads in which are possible to get there. I was told you do not always have to hold a conversation with them yet watch and follow the ways in which they communicate to the world, what worked for them and what did not. I was told they may never know you and for that reason may never be in a position to validate you yet they provide you with solid training from afar via their passion and expertise of their craft or God given works. Did you know you can train by simply watching the life of another? We are a conglomerate of who we chose and some we don't (giggle) modeled, shaped, molded and aligned with the many souls that will cross the pathways of our lives whether it be through church, T.V., radio, books, our jobs and or affiliates, family and or friends. Choose Wisely.

Cindy Trimm

The beauty and power you possess is breathtaking; Your sell out for God like no other. Your books too have helped me in some of the darkest of dark moments in my life. They caused me to look at my life just a bit closer. They empowered me to learn about God and revisit just who He has created us to be, who He has designed us to be and what He has intended for us to be able to do. I always feel ten feet taller after reading a book you have written. You cannot go wrong following a leader who is following God and that you are most definitely doing! To call out every demon, warlock, imp and ism with no bone of fear in your body, no ounce of waiver in your soul, no question in your spirit and no flinch in your flesh, in one of the most tenacious manners I have ever known is beyond admirable. It is War fare at its best. As I have said before…when you look for mentors in your life, you look for the best of the best. You have a passion for truth, life and purpose. Thank you for sharing with the world that there truly is a "MORNING" and that we CAN COMMAND IT for ourselves by simply opening our mouth, speaking life and not death, truth not lies, victory not defeat and letting our light outshine the dark. Your life's work has made me excited to walk the walk, talk the talk and stay committed to fasting as I fall to refocus, get back on track and attack! I pray a shield and covering of protection over your life as you seek expose the enemy for the liar that he is and bring us closer to the love of our life…Jesus Christ! Amen

Steve Harvey

When you can stand in adversity and say "Hey, I am only human" and still have the courage to face the world……..WOW! Mr. Harvey. I want to say Reverend Harvey, you have inspired me with your heart. You have found a way to use the vehicle in which you were given to spread the word world- wide. Now that's power! That's courage! That's love! To care enough to use your platform to share an encouraging word to the world...My God. It speaks volumes. Your character, charisma, courage and love for Christ are to be contended with. Thank you. You stand as a role model to my son and I am ever so grateful.

President Barack Obama and First Lady Michelle Obama
To my President Barack Obama... Yes we can! Yes we did! Yes I will continue to do! Your leadership speaks for itself. Thank you. Thank you for your countless acts of courage. This entire book represents what we can do if we take the steps of faith that have already been paved out for us. Your steps definitely have added to clearing the way. You have given light to what some may have considered impossible and made possible a visible sight of what could only be seen in the longing of a hopeful heart. My son now has a vision of just what he can look forward to if he puts his best foot forward. May God bless your next steps and cover your life and the life of your entire family.

To my First Lady Michelle Obama...
"Girl of the South Side". I hesitate even writing this as my words are so elementary in regard to the description you are truly deserving of having written or publicized. Uncommon Grace you most definitely carry. You represent everything I stand for and look forward to; motherhood, business woman, educator, orator, world- wide leader, wife and so much more. Thank you.

You have weathered a many a storm over a many of years and made it look like a day on the beach. Now that's grace. Your beauty, your class, your elegance and ability to relate to the common in us all,~leaves me speechless. I reach for a word that encompasses it all. I cannot find one. There is a God, when you can turn on the t.v. and see yourself in your own first lady. What more to say but again, Thank you.

Oprah~

Your life speaks volumes! I don't know you but I know you~for you have allowed the world in to your soul. Thank you for the passionate spirit you possess! Thank you for the boldness you embody to stand as a woman, a black woman. You do not shrink to the limits the world has set for us. Moreover you have broken through the strongholds set on our lives with an uncommon grace. I don't speak to your money for money comes and money goes but to that in which you represent. Thank you for setting the bar so high that I had that I had to get up and leap for it! I accepted the call, challenge and opportunity God has so graciously given unto me to get up another day and express myself to the world as I continue to press toward the mark of a higher calling! Thank you for displaying how one can do all things through Christ who is our strength. Thank you for showing me that I too can do this even as a single woman.

Bishop T.D. Jakes ~

Man of God thank you! To set yourself free is one thing. To set a people free is yet another. But to set a woman free is selfless and personal to my walk, my destiny and my life. Because of your obedience to God, your willingness to acknowledge us and present our struggle as one that is relevant and worthy of restoration~ MANY WOMEN have been set free! What a priceless gift to be bestowed upon us! # FREEDOM! I can only pray my contribution makes a portion of the difference yours has made on the life of women who have been bound and yearned to be loosed!

Penny Armstrong, Jo Anne McCarthy, Trista Brown, Rhonda Cotton, Alnisa Tower, Mellissa Billeci-Spikes, Carrie Sullivan, Elizabeth Hunter, Niki Davis, Niki Givens, Rochelle Cole, Evangelist Yvette Mc Henry, Kathy Flennaugh NaTasha Brown, Alinzia Hughes, Minister Ornicia Lowe, Marilyn Jeffers, Anna Reyes Shepherd, Dr. Lakita Long, Cheri Whitehead, Minister Merthia Caston, Linda Wicker-Johnson, Minister Candace Hunter, Kamilah Shani Mayo, Minister Ornicia Lowe,Minister Hadassah, Erika Newton, Kizzy Gay.

Sisters...

The book would never end if I thanked each of you individually. Can I say that in my darkest hours of life I called on God and each time He sent angels. How do I know this?....Because when I looked up I saw your faces. You all never asked me for a dime to compensate for all you have done for me and my family. People, without going in to details, these ladies have thrown baby showers when I was so ashamed and thought I had no one, fed my children, housed me (again without request for money) picked up my children, kept them safe for me, encouraged me in the Lord, prayed with me, yanked me up out of my misery, cleaned my house, held my hand, sent financial blessings left and right that kept my hotel bills paid, lights on, phone on, gas in my tank and toys under the tree and stayed up ALL night with me as midwives through my birthing process. Yes, there are men that have helped and brothers I Thank you too~ but it's nothing like a sister that even in the midst of her struggle gives of herself to ensure the vitality of life in another sister. That's love and this goes for my step sister Aimee Fields and my blood sister Heather Strange- Lenz as well. I not only thank you all, but... I LOVE YOU!

It can be a scary place to have vision when no one else can see it. It can also be a very vulnerable place as well. Sharing your vision leaves you exposed, naked and left wide open for scrutiny, doubt, shame and discouragement if what you see doesn't come to fruition. In these moments you need a safe cover, a place to openly dream, a team of cheerleaders to propel you forward no matter what it looks like. You need someone to believe in you with no condemnation; someone excited to see the end results of what even you are unsure of. This next group of people, have done just that for me. Whether they just sat and listened for hours lol some overnight to my Kooky ideas, added advice or even rolled up their sleeves to physically and financially make it happen, none of what I may have accomplished would have manifested without the safety of their friendship nor energy exerted in the things they have done to help propel my vision forward. What you may have experienced in sharing this journey with me via my book, photos or cd you experienced because of these individuals. These individuals heard and saw in the spirit before any of this even existed. In fact it was their belief, encouragement, love and action that helped me to get here!

To my friends and family that have seen me at my highest of highs and remained through the lowest of my lows. Thank you for loving me, believing in me, opening doors for me, staying by my side and praying me right on through this thang', allowing me to cry on your shoulders, stay in your homes, bringing me food and clothing, speaking into and over my life and praying:

My sentiments are shared with you. You all are prayer warriors straight from heaven and I am forever grateful. We sowed in tears but shall reap in joy! I love you all.

Thank you, my friend ~ Thor Bartzi

Anthony Lowe and Ornicia Lowe: My power couple producers, Jim Payton: Book cover photographer ,Hank Hicks, James FoxIII, Grandma Fannie Fox, Bishop Navelle Rufus, Deacon John Berry, Minister Jesse Dangerfield, Rodney Jones,(nicca), Ray Evans, Erik Big E Gibson, Pastor A.J. Johnson, Kevin Varitek, Vernitta Ninah Weddles, Kizzie Gay, Tameika Lee, Dr Nakita Denise Thomas –Allen, Bishop L.E. Franklin, Lamont Jackson, Lil Ronn Rosson, Shawn and Rio Golden, Chaney, Joe love, Ernest Dayce, Rachel Gould, Mel Robinson, Rev. William Ward, Clarence Shells, Terry Blinks, Quintenella Huffman, Donneshia, Tasha Russel, Shauny B, Jeremy Ruelos, A.J. Ruelos, Alberto Vega, James, Rhonda, Gina, Michael Madison, Maurice Williams, Dave Russel, Bishop Keith Henderson,Minister Candace Hunter, Nashone Holmes, Stacie McCay, George Miller, John Kravarik Pastor Felix Golden, W. Clemente Sheppard, Minister Nicole, Minister Billie-Joe Wright Robinson, Melissa Billeci-Spikes, Alnisa Tower, Chester Brooks, Laura Babbit, Evangelist Ore, Minister Miles Minnick and Lady Tina, Samuel Ayoko, Rio Golden, Seth, Charles Guy, T'Shaun Taylor, David Dodson, David Clark III, David Scott, Derrick DeWaun

Williams, Isaiah Williams, Brent Taylor, Nick Lee Jr., Deaconess Lacey, Deorah Howard, Sonja Honeycutt, Pastor and wife Juan Castro, Pastor Inga Mork, Pastor Inga, Pastor, Minister Sean Franklin, George and Bethany Jordan, Kenneth Brown, Domonic Lynch, Lorraine Stewart, Lorraine Williams, Claudia, Kevin Johnson, Janitha Hall, Karen McDuffie, Ariel, Daytrese, Cheryl, Ebony, Cristian Kuria, Benton, Marquise, Marquevius Temmons, Blessing, Pastor Hinkle, Nic Lee, Johnathan Williams, Redd, Pastor David Evans, Minister Mike Jones, Vernon Hall, Mystro, Richard Tucker, Calvin Dunn, Hellen-Gill Smith, Jacoree Prothro, Terry Flennaugh, Andre Bratcher Gloria Dodson, Dawaun King, Elizabeth Hunter, Jeremy Bardswell, Erika Newton, Stephanie Jackson.

Charles Guy, Trista Brown, Rhonda Cotton, Penny Armstrong, JoAnne McCarthy (UIC Hoop PHI Women's Basketball Team and all the athletic teams, coaches and professors); Clarence Shells, T'Shaun Taylor, James Fox III, John Kravarik, Kevin Varitek, Amelia Bowerman, Reggie Murray, NaTasha Brown, Yolanda Mcghee, Nikki Givens, Niki Davis, David Marquis Young, Don Scott, Michael Madison, Kizzy Gay, George Miller, Alnisa Tower, Melissa Belecci, Rodney Jones, Mario Golden, Johnelle Slone, Anthony Caldwell, Rebecca Gonzo, LuciAntonio, Blessing D., Joleen D., Chad the Dad Brisco, Alinzia Davenport, Michael Lampley, Ornicia and Anthony Lowe, Claudia McCree, Angela Abrea, Marcus Cadet, Seed of

Faith Family, Rock of Ages family, New Birth family, Tameka Harris and Liz Head, Aria Kinswell, Michael Lampley, Sherell Ford, Ryan Brinkley, Byron Foster, Rochelle Cole, VernittaWeddles, Dr. Lakita Long, Timbo, Ayesha Viaan, Minister Nicole Forward, Minister Hadassah Thomas, Minister Curtis Thomas, Minister Stephanie Wakefield, Deacon Ralph and Alma Palmer, my Judah family, Elder Ron Rosson, King Dawaun, Elizabeth (Lizzy) Hunter, Pastor Anthony Johnson, Linda Wicker- Johnson, MerthiaSaeed, Mama Candace Hunter, Marilyn Jeffers, Cheri Whitehead, Lamont Jackson, Ron Rosson Jr., Min. Chantell Rosson, Bishop Franklin, Pastor Jerry Pedock, All of my players and students over the years, Thor Bartzi, Minister Mike Jones, Stacie Parrish, Room 7, Tasha Russell, Donesha Thomas, Jeremy and A.J. Ruelos, Steve, A.J. Cassie, Jillian, Quin, Saka, Roxanne, Nate, Alberto Vega, Tony and Toni, Rhonda and James Sadlab, Denae, KiKi, Amber, Sandy, Nicole Mikhail, Cheryl, Yohat, Jeniffer, Sarah, Terita, Karen, Sarah, Danielle P., Margret, Janitha, XTIGONE adult cast - Awele, Naima, Howard, Ryan, Tavia, A.J., Michael, Drew, and Dwight Mahabir, Safira, Brenda, Jo Anne, Niru, Margie Wells, Danielle, Robert Crawley, Yvette Mchenry, Nashone Holmes, Minister Kasey, Dante' Sims, Minister Jesse Dangerfield, Kamilah Turner, Jim Payton, Mazella and Phillip Houston, Pastor Stacie Smith, Elder Ray Ressler and Danielle Ressler, Bernadette Silva, Keisha Frowner, Pastor Kay, Minister Billie

Joe, Pastor Bessie Corgille, Bishop Lamar Collins, Tanya Friend, Sarah Hernandez., Sarah Black., Angela Abrea, Angela and Laurie, Minister Cheryl Sweat, Minister Kacy, Bishop Isreal Monroe, Dr. Jerry Rice, Rockridge Safeway/Starbucks, Bishop Mc Neal, David Clark, Pastor David Evans, Brent Taylor, Isaiah Williams, Todd Dulaney, Minister Deandre' Patterson, Elder Paulette Harper, Carmeleta Belt, Mrs. Asselin, (God son) Trenton, Sharonda Wheat, Sharonda Major, Diane Major, Leasa Heart, Ken Hunter, Ken Dominick Metz, Bishop Carlton Leonard, Pastor and lady Philandrew Miller, Shaunricka Sien-colon, David Clark, Bishop R.D. Garrison, Stacie McKay, Neal Read Records and Publishing, L.E. Franklin Records, Clinton, Cousin Rhonda Mckirven, Gino, Katherine and Maria (Cheena), Tanisha (Ki) , Pastor Sid Burrows, Bethany and George Jordan. Obysco Obysco clothing, Minister Shirly Gaines, Byrd sisters and family, Jay Larry, Jay, Coach Lane, India Little, Rhodessa Jones, Naima Grace, Michael, Ryan, Andrew, Mohabir, Awele, A.J., Dance Choreographer, Katie Nowaski, PACIFIC BOYCHOIR ACADEMY, PITTSBURG HIGHSCHOOL and district, Pittsburg Community Theatre, African American Shakespeare Co./ Theatre, Bishop (The Ship), Abundant life Church membersBobbie and A.J. Anderson, Kaitlyn, Morayo, Sequoia, Cyesha, Falon Jones, Nandi and Asamaad Robison, Marleah and Marjenae, Tatiana and Ben, Angel Blocker, Joi Lanzy, Lamara Whitley, Pastor and Lady Lanzy, Minister Sean and Lady Olga Franklin, Shaunricka Sien-Colon, Lady LeKeisha Nord(Jr. high besties) and Amy Bowerman (elementary school bestie):

Pastor Lita Colon, Terry and Kathy Flennaugh, Lady Shaday and Pastor Marcus Taylor, Tashaka, Tiffany, Pastors Chantell and Damon Owens, Pastor Bridges, Bronche', Korie, Denise Bridges, Pastor Bryce, Pastor Chris and Joyce Willis, Bishop Willis, Terry Blinks, Derrick, Michael Madison, Pastor Miles Minick and Lady Tina Minnick, Pastors Tim and David Manly, Pastor Perkins, Christian K., Ariel, Marilyn, Daytrese, Cheryl, Bishop Keith Henderson, Aaron Baugh, Rich Bentley, Pastor Henry and lady Denise Dillihant, Minister Alyssa Jackson, Awele Makeba, Terrence Chandler, David Jackson, Lamar Hildreth, Tony, Terry Blinks, Richard Tucker, Lady, Pastor and Lady Quivander Kirkland-Smith, J Red, Adam Olgy, Tommy James Sheppard Jr. Pastot Chantell Rosson, Pastor Romell Williiams, Pastor Garrison, Pastor Bullock, Seth Roberson, Ashley, Mel Roberson, Donte' , Star, Laquishe, Carrie Saravia, Catherine Stevens, Amber, Ebony, Tj Fox, Debora Williams, Robert Crawely Sr., Natasha, Mike and Min. Jason Crawely, Dr. Rejoice Frazier-Meyer, Pastor Howe- Antioch Church Family, Pastor Michelle Hadassah, Pastor Larry Blueford, Pastor Jonny Riley, Apostle Cynthia Chess, Apostle Liddel, Bishop Ernestine Reems, Pastor Timothy Hinkle, Pastor Kelly Woods, Sylvia Smith, Kriss Ross, Donte' Sims, Min. Nina Carter, Min. Rodney

Blanchard, April Mason, Sylvia Smith, Char Louise, C Ninah Lentz, Diatra Simpson, Pastor Tiffany James, Pastor Maurice and Lady Bates, Cousin Jr. Riley and family, Carrie Anne, Bronche', Bishop and Pastor Shirley Gains, Minister Delmar and lady Johnson, Janeen, Janine, Martin Santiago, The Martins, Lady Carol and Pastor Harris Pleasant Grove, Pastor Joy, Pastor Monica Gort, Pastor Inga Mork, "BLACK", Terris Chandler, Shamika, Kimari, kameron, Ashley, Joi, Jr. Lanzy Jessica, Anna Reyes Shepherd, Pittsburg High Basketball, coach Lane, coach Gali, Chery Neal Reed, L. E. Franklin Records, Queen mother and the Royal family, Pastor Kingston Bullen, Pastor Freda Mitchell, Riccol Johnson, Mike Mitzel, Corey Page "The Poet", Germaine Daniels, Pastor Brandon Walter, Pastor Anthony L. Perkins, Pastor Blackman and family, Pastor and lady Angie Alvarado, Mazella Houston, Mr. Houston, Lanesha Morris, Lady Lanitra and Pastor Gerald lanzy, Sharon and Mo Jones, Cina Gable, Pastor Santos Howard, Pastor Anthony Blackmon, Velma Foxx, Rachel, Pastors Castro, Rachel Castro Escorcia, Jerica Castro, Pastor Henry L. Perkins, Pastor Steve Vaugn, April Foster, Karen Gasken, Calvin Dunn, Kevin Johnson, Sylvia Smith, Bernadette Silva and family, Faafiti family, Dawana, Mic, Kim, Marie, Christina, Rita, Easter Raven, Shaniqua, Kathy, Cindy, Ayesha, Thandi, Wanda Ali Batin Sabir, Oakland Post, Minister Ali and wife, Elder Heather, Aunt Odessa, Dr. Orange' and staff, Minister Oscar and Carol Jones, Pastors Shaun and

Dianna Nepstad Fellowship Church, The Glickmans, Marianela and Conzaga, Brth Torres, Omar Staples, Cedric, Catalina, Fabrisio Elavancini cousin Anthony Stingily and mom Bernadine, Cee Bee, Stephan Waters, Rashid Culp, Betty Shavers, Sportt Smith, Prophett Raymond Kelly, Nancy Trieber, Kevin Lenz, Lorrain and John Berry, Renee' Ussery, April Foster, UIC Staff and WOMEN'S BASKETBALL PROGRAM, Loyola University Women's Basketball program, Chicago State Women's Basketball program, Robert Morris Women's Basketball program, Antioch Grocery Outlet Managers Dwayne and Linda Burns, Rockridge Safeway/ Starbucks staff and manager Carl.

Gloria Dodson, Minister David Dodson, Minister Billie Joe, Minister Jeremy Bardwell, Dr. Greg Sephus, Francisco Diaz, Richard Tucker, Ray Evans, Dr. Patrick Weaver, David Scott, Keith Pace, Step-Dad Ernie Fields, James Jr. Pops, Gramma Fannie, Tim, Ebony and Amber Fox, Truvella, Helen-Gill, Jacoree Prothro, Shauna, Joseph B. Washington, Elder Gail Knowles, Elder Heather Dawson, Elder Charlie Florin, Minister Sheila, Minister Karla Allen, Usef Surney, Antonio and Tia Allen, Minister Shaun and Olga Franklin, Tanya Friend, Erika Newton, Bernadette Silva, Minister Cheryl Sweat, Minister Kim Davis, Pastor Sarah Morgan, Elder French'nette Bryant, Elder Claude Lang, Pastor Erik Gillette and family, Minister Kacey Threats and family, Pastor David Evans, D.C Clark, Prophetess

Reign Johnson, Mychal Stanford, Pastor Erick Gillette and family, Eric Bigg Gipson, Federal D. Glover, Pastor Castro and family, My brother and sister Heather Strange-Lenz, brother in – law Kevin Lenz, Alonzo Strange III, Grandmother Jesse Lacey Strange, Ellis family, Pastor Gerald and Lanitra Lanzy and family, Nana Coston, George and Bethany Coston, Kathy and Terry Flennaugh, Christine Flynn, Lorrain Stewart, Hilda Porter, Dee-Dee Wahliq, Ray and Willie Jane Mathenia, Shauny B. Smith, Angela and Lori, Gill, Nina, Shannon, niece, Johnelle, Anthony Caldwell, Rachel Gould, Deacon John and Lasundra Berry, Pastor, Sharronda Wheat, Germaine Daniels, Minister Deborah Abraham Howard, The Honeycutts, Emerald Brown, AnetteNatt, Pastor and Lady Qwivander Smith, Johnny Morney Jr., Pastor Mapp, Nambi E. Kelley, Sandi, Safira M., Pastor and First Lady William and Roshunda Ward, Minister Bobbie Ward, Ron Wilbourn, Ernest Dayce, Pastors Philip and Janice Butler, Vanessa Williams, Minister Cy and Edwina Forh, Minister Alisa Jackson, Corey Page, Dr. Renee Winston, Connie Cooper, Elizabeth Cooper, Toni Keene-Manago, Angelo Winston, 9 Quota Awards, Tanicia Shamay Currie, Shauny B. Smith, B. Pierre (Nasty), Marie Thornton, Kayla Gonzalez, Pastor Bessie Corgile, Dr. Apostle Christine Liddell, Jasmine Romes, Aunt Michelle Lawson-Baily, Pastor Navelle Rufus, Bishop Marc Neal, Pastor Karlton Ray, Karen Gaskin, Shauna McKneeley, Trish Nickolas, Yvette Papillon, Germaine Danielle Evans, Leon

Timbo, In memory of Deacon Anderson and family, Deacon Battle and family and Betty Ellis and family, Deaconess Lacey and family, Tanya Williams, Cousin Rhonda, Kevin Johnson, Kevin McCoy, Terry Blinks, Dodye Lord Lloyd, Rhonda Marvell, Ben, Julious, Ernie, Calvin Dunn, Angela Abrea and family, Richard Gonzalez and family, Ellis family, Bishop Eddie Wright, Pastor Eugene Jackson, Rashid Culp, Pastor Romell Williams, Hank Hicks, Antonette Bryant, Sacheen Thompson and family, Charmagne, E.B. Works, cousin Anthony Stingily and mom Bernadine, Cee Bee, Stephan Waters, Rashid Culp, Marlott and Mrs. Williams, Pleasant Grove Baptist Church, Pastor Thomas HarrisIII and lady Carol, Nancy Trieber, Kevin Lenz and family, Lorrain and John Berry, Renee' Ussery, April Foster, UIC Staff and WOMEN'S BASKETBALL PROGRAM, Loyola University Women's Basketball program, Chicago State Women's Basketball program, Robert Morris Women's Basketball program, India Little, Evelyn Dillard, Antioch Grocery Outlet Managers Dwayne and Linda Burns, Rockridge Safeway/ Starbucks staff and manager Carl, Revy Rev's.

William Sheppard, Don Sheppard, Papa Ben, half-sister Aimee Fields, half-brother Daniel Fields, Cindy Manly Fields, Step Father Earnie Fields~(Thank you for loving me like your own); my aunts and uncles: Deborah, Adilisha (Marla) (Uncle Agili Hodari), Jackie, Paula Yvette (Uncle Jim), Bonnie Gloria-Helen, Richard (Aunt Carmen), Cheri; all of my cousins and their

296

families Kafele, Rashidi, Simba, Safiya, Ahimsa, Jake, Simon, Abigail, Kimille, Oscar, Aaron, Cameron, Princeton and…. (the Stingily family extended…)

I have never thanked the family for taking me in, nor their teenage now adult daughter for allowing me to share her parents. Thank you Tameka Harris Mrs. Liz Head and Mr. Gene Head!

Shanene Higgins: Woman of God. What can I say? Thank you! It's been a long time coming. You never gave up on me. You saw something in my work and over road business with Jesus. You understood that there was a message that needed to get out and you saw fit to make it happen. Your professionalism is uncanny. You encouraged me *all* the way through. You are not only a publisher but a midwife as well! The birthing room is a very special place. Few are allowed in. I am glad that you were in the room along my side helping to push this book out! I am amazed at the God in you and look forward to many more partnerships with you

~ Eyes on top of eyes are needed when putting out a product of this magnitude, birthed from your belly and released into the world's atmosphere. Not only are there few you trust to handle your baby, but few who care the way you do about it.

These two women of God I cannot repay for the help they have given me…Help that would cost thousands to a publishing company, not only did I read it, but they read it, not only did I type it but they edited on top of my edits and typed on top of my typing to ensure the greatest quality and outcome the four of us could possibly produce. Smooches~ smooches. God loves you for this and I absolutely adore you both. My decision to self-publish was quite frightening after the comfort of first putting the project all in the hands of a professional Christian publishing company, Higgins Publishing (Shanene Higgins) who spent countless hours beautifully formatting, advising and structuring my book to the point where editing was all that we had left to do. However, the amount of work left was overwhelming for me to say the least. I found comfort in my soul when God sent these next two angels, Minister Stephanie Jackson (my final eyes and hands of editing) and Recording Artist Erika Lotus Newton who dropped the final book in to publishing, reformatting and typing in ALL of the edits I'd put in before and after Minister Jackson put in all of her as well. Countless hours each of these women spent to make sure this book would find itself into your hands, houses and hearts to heal the heavy from heaven. The four of us represent what Kingdom looks like if you ask me. Thank you to each of you for lending yourself unto God. I know it was for God because….Well, you know…smile

~IN LOVING MEMORY OF~

Grandfather Alonzo Strange Sr. (Bunky) Grandmother Hattye Stingily, Grandfather Clyde Stingily, Auntie Debra Stingily, "Pops", Don Sheppard, "poppy", James Fox III, Jarren King, Marrio Golden, David Johnson, Timothy Fox , Monique Nicole Maeberry, Rolfe Crumpler, Jerrin King, Uncle Jr., Chauncy Baily Oakland Tribune, Bishop Eddie Long and all precious lives gone on to glory before us ...

Jasmine Tamara Romes

Selfless beauty like none I have ever witnessed… Your strength and love unmatched…You would be so very proud of me. Thank you for loving me, standing up for me and including my son into your life. We love and miss you dearly. When I sit down to read, I will curl up and call on you from heaven to read, laugh and cry with me like you used to. Rest in Heaven

"ALL MY LOVE"

Time doesn't quite align

With the plans we have in our minds

Life even in faith

Brings us to a place we all must face

I'll never erase your beautiful face

The sound of your voice fills this empty space

Now you are gone , I'm tryna hold on

I've got to be strong, for you I'll go on

But now I wonder how

I'm going to make it without your smile

I wonder when my heart will ever mend again

All my love I send

I'd do it again Just to hold your hand

I'd do it all again

My pride and joy my baby boy

I'd do it all again

You were my world, my baby girl

Ooooo oooo oooo ooooo

Ooooo oooo oooo ooooo

I don't comprehend, father please send

Your comforting hand, Lord your will and your plan

Angel your free, though living in me

I feel your heartbeat

Now you can soar forever more

To God I owe you Everything..... Thank you for the incredible gift of life which I give back to you and amazing opportunity to serve your people and bless your name! May your light continually shine through me ~love your daughter ~ Jasmine

www.ingramcontent.com/pod-product-compliance
Lightning Source LLC
Chambersburg PA
CBHW061424040426
42450CB00007B/888